Collins · *do brilliantly !*

CW00376431

Test**Practice**

KS3 Science

Test practice at its **best**

■ **Steven Goldsmith**

■ **Series Editor: Jayne de Courcy**

Contents

About the Science National Tes

When is the Test?

You will sit your Science National Test in May of Year 9. Your teacher will give you the exact dates.

What does the Test cover?

The science curriculum is divided into four Attainment Targets. The test covers all four of these:

Sc1 Scientific Enquiry
Sc2 Life Processes and Living Things
Sc3 Materials and their Properties
Sc4 Physical Properties

From 2003 there has been an increase in the number of questions that assess scientific enquiry (Sc
These questions may be in the context of any of the other science attainment targets as well as askin
direct questions about Sc1. These may be in rather unusual contexts, which do not require any specif
scientific knowledge but ask you to demonstrate your understanding of the processes involved in scien
investigations.

There may be whole or part questions based on scientific enquiry and you will be expected to show ho
well you understand scientific terms such as fair testing and independent variable. Questions in the tes
may ask you to explain:

- how an investigation could be carried out;
- what factors need to be controlled;
- what factors need to be measured;
- whether the outcome can be predicted;
- how the results are going to be presented;
- what the results show and whether they match the predictions;
- the outcome and whether the evidence collected is significant, reliable and valid.

There are many examples of these types of questions in this book. They are identified clearly in t
'**What's this question looking for?**' section of the Answers and Comments.

How many papers are there?

You take two Test papers – Paper 1 and Paper 2.
Both papers include questions on all four Attainment Targets.

The Test papers are set at two different tiers:

The tiers overlap and some of the questions are the same across the tiers.

LEVEL	LEVEL	LEVEL	LEVEL
3	4	5	6

If you take the Tier 3-6 paper, you can achieve a level 3, 4, 5 or 6. If you take the Tier 5-7 paper, you can achieve a level 5, 6 or 7. Your teacher will decide which tier will best allow you to show what you know and understand about Science.

LEVEL	LEVEL	LEVE
5	6	7

What is a good grade?

By the end of Key Stage 3, most pupils have attained between levels 3 and 7. A typical 14 year-old will achieve a level 5 or 6 in their National Test.

Exceptional performance	●	considerably better than the expected lev
Level 8	●	
Level 7	●	better than the expected level
Level 6	●	expected level for 14 year olds
Level 5	●	
Level 4	●	
Level 3	●	working towards the expected level
Level 2	●	
Level 1	●	
Age	**14 years**	

How to do well in your Test

1 Practise the right tier – no Test surprises

This book contains a complete Paper 1 and a complete Paper 2 at **both tiers**. It is clearly marked where each tier begins and ends. Only complete the questions for the appropriate tier.

Your teacher will tell you which tier you will be entered for. You can then work through the complete Paper 1 and Paper 2 for that tier.

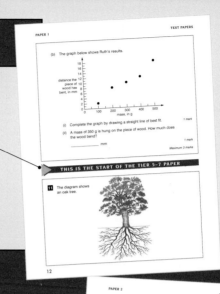

2 Answers and Comments – to boost your grade

Detailed comments are given in addition to the correct answer for each question.

This means that if you get an answer wrong, you will be able to see where you went wrong and learn what to do next time.

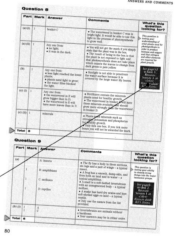

3 'What the examiner wants' – inside help from the experts

In the 'What's this question looking for?' section, there is even more help. This tells you exactly which Science concept or skill the question was written to test. It also tells you which chapter of *Collins Revision Guide KS3 Science* will help you with the topic.

4 Practise working under Test conditions

● Choose somewhere quiet to work while you are doing the test.
● Make sure you have everything you need: pen, pencil, rubber, ruler, protractor and calculator.
● In the Test you will be allowed 1 hour to complete each paper. To get used to working under timed conditions, don't spend more than 1 hour on each paper.
● Leave time to check your answers carefully within the 1 hour.

If you use this book properly, it will give you the best possible preparation for your actual Test – and help you achieve your best Test score.

How to calculate your level

To find out what level you have achieved, add up the marks you got for Papers 1 and 2.

The table below shows you the marks for each level at each tier. (N means no level awarded.)

Level	Tier 3–6	Tier 5–7
N	0–33	0–35
2	34–40	
3	41–71	
4	72–103	36–41
5	104–132	42–72
6	133+	73–104
7		105+

Paper 1

1 The drawings show eight living things.

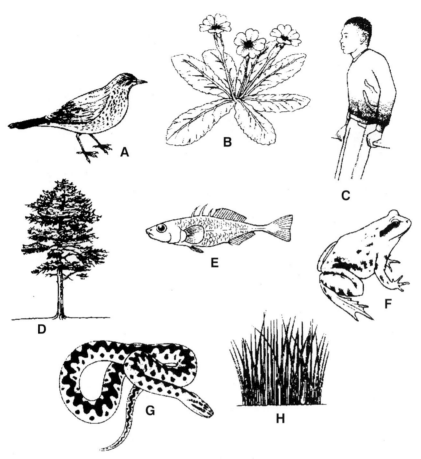

Give the letters of:

(a) **one** living thing which uses gills to take in oxygen;   1 mark

(b) **one** living thing which produces seeds;   1 mark

(c) **one** living thing which uses lungs to breathe;   1 mark

(d) **two** living things which lay eggs in water;

.... and .... 2 marks

(e) **two** living things which are covered in scales.

.... and .... 2 marks

Maximum 7 marks

2 Two pupils planted lettuce seeds at three different temperatures.
They planted the same number of seeds at each temperature.

Their results are shown in the table.

temperature, in °C	total number of lettuce seeds germinated					
	day 1	day 2	day 3	day 4	day 5	day 6
5	0	0	--------	0	1	1
15	0	0	0	1	5	9
25	0	2	8	13	17	19

(a) Complete the table to show how many seeds had germinated at 5°C by day 3.

1 mark

(b) The pupils were trying to find out something about seeds.
Write down the question the pupils were investigating.

....

.... *1 mark*

(c)   The pupils discussed their results and made the conclusions listed below.
       Look at their results in the table and decide whether each conclusion below is
       true, **false** or you **cannot tell**.
       Tick the correct box for each conclusion.   *2 marks*

conclusions	**true**	**false**	**cannot tell**
The earliest germination was at 25°C.	☐	☐	☐
At 25°C all the seeds germinated by day 6.	☐	☐	☐
5°C was too cold for seeds to germinate.	☐	☐	☐
The best temperature for germination was 15°C.	☐	☐	☐

Maximum 4 marks

3   The diagram below shows an organ system in the human body.

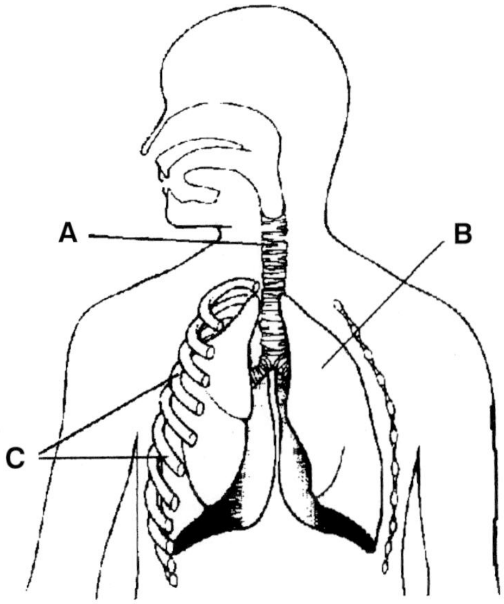

(a)   What is the name of the organ system shown in the diagram?
       Tick the correct box.

       circulatory system   ☐   reproductive system   ☐

       digestive system   ☐   respiratory system   ☐

1 mark

(b)   What are the names of parts A and B?

part A   ....

part B   ....   *2 marks*

(c)   Parts C are bones which support the chest. Give the name of these bones.

....   *1 mark*

(d)   The photograph shows a man using a sanding machine on a piece of wood.
He is wearing a mask to stop him from breathing in the sawdust.

The mask has tiny holes in it.

(i)   When the man breathes in, the mask separates particle of sawdust from the air.
What is this method of separation called?

....   *1 mark*

(ii)   If the man breathed in the particles of sawdust what might happen to him?

....

....   *1 mark*

Maximum 6 marks

4 (a) Many chemicals are dangerous if not used carefully.
Read the **two** hazard descriptions. Look at the hazard labels.
Draw a line from each description to the correct label.

hazard labels

P   Q   R   S   T

POISONOUS This will cause damage if swallowed	CORROSIVE This can attack or dissolve many things

hazard descriptions   *2 marks*

(b) The label on a bottle of kitchen cleaner says:

It leaves kitchen and bathroom surfaces bright and shiny.

Another part of the label says:

Contains sulphuric acid
Irritating to eyes and skin
Keep out of reach of children

(i) The chart shows the colour of universal indicator in different solutions.

type of solution	strongly acidic	weakly acidic	neutral	weakly alkaline	strongly alkaline
colour of universal indicator	red	orange	green	blue	purple

What colour will the kitchen cleaner turn universal indicator?

---   *1 mark*

(ii) Which hazard label do you expect to see on the bottle?
Write the correct letter from the list above.

---   *1 mark*

Maximum 4 marks

5   Different metals are used to make different things.

(a)   Draw lines to match each metal to **one** use and to **one** property which makes the metal good for that use.

3 marks

metal	use	property
aluminium	racing bicycle frames	does not react easily
gold	compass needle	lightweight
steel	jewellery	magnetic

(b)   A pipe for hot water is made from copper wrapped in plastic foam.

(i)   Which property makes copper suitable for making pipes for hot water? Tick the correct box.

Copper is a shiny metal. ☐

Copper is a good conductor of heat. ☐

Copper does **not** react with water. ☐

Copper is a good conductor of electricity. ☐

1 mark

(ii)   Why is plastic foam used to wrap hot water pipes?

--- *1 mark*

Maximum 5 marks

6 Sean placed some ice cubes in a beaker in a warm room.

The total mass of the ice cubes was 40 g.

(a) What mass of water is formed when all the ice has melted?

-------------------------------------- g   *1 mark*

(b) After three days, only half of the water was left in the beaker.
(i) What had happened to the other half of the water?

---   *1 mark*

(ii) After just one more day there was no more water left in the beaker.
Give **two** ways the conditions in the room changed to make this happen
so quickly.

1 ---

2 ---   *2 marks*

Maximum 4 marks

7 (a) Joseph and Meena did some experiments to show how new rocks
can be formed.

(i) Joseph used the following materials.

sand   pebbles   water   plaster

Joseph mixed these materials and left the mixture to go hard.
The solid looked like this.

Rocks are grouped into three types: **igneous**, **metamorphic** and
sedimentary.

Which of these types of rock is most like Joseph's 'rock'?

--   *1 mark*

(ii) Meena took some crystals. She put them in a crucible and heated it until the crystals melted. She let the crucible cool very slowly until the contents went solid. The solid she tipped out from the crucible looked like this.

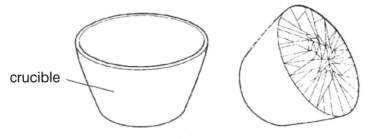

crucible

Which of the three types of rock is most like Meena's 'rock'?

-- *1 mark*

(b) Rocks can be broken by weathering when:

1 Water gets into cracks in rocks.
2 The water in the cracks turns to ice and expands.
3 The rocks split into smaller pieces.

What else must happen during this part of this weathering process?
Tick **two** boxes.

The temperature stays the same. ☐

The temperature falls below freezing point. ☐

The temperature stays above freezing point. ☐

Expansion forces the cracks in the rock to close. ☐

Expansion forces the cracks in the rock to open. ☐

Expansion forces all of the water out of the cracks. ☐

2 marks

Maximum 4 marks

8 Lee blew across the top of paper tubes to make sounds.
    He investigated how changing the length of a tube affects the pitch of the sound.

(a) What equipment could he use to measure the length of the tubes?
    Tick the correct box.

1 mark

(b) The photograph on the right
    shows the different lengths of
    tubes Lee used.

Suggest **one** way his test might **not** have been fair.

--- *1 mark*

(c) Lee made a prediction.

Which of these statements is a prediction?
    Tick the correct box.

The tubes were made of paper.

The pitch of the sound is how high or low it is.

The longer tube will make a lower sound.

The sound is caused by the vibration of air.   *1 mark*

(d)   Lee blew across the ends of 3 different lengths of tube and compared the pitch of the sound produced.

His results are shown below.

Length of the tube, in cm	pitch of the sound
5	high
25	medium
50	low

Which length of tube made the sound with the highest pitch?

-------------------------------------- cm   *1 mark*

Maximum 4 marks

9   Thunder and lightning happen at the same time.

(a)   We see the flash of lightning before we hear the thunder.
       Give the reason for this.

---   *1 mark*

(b)   Omar investigated the movement of a storm. He measured the time between seeing a flash of lightning and hearing the thunder.
       He did this six times. Omar put his results in a table.

flash of lightning	time between seeing the lightning and hearing the thunder, in seconds
A	8.0
B	5.0
C	3.0
D	9.0
E	13.0
F	16.5

Omar drew a bar chart of his results as shown below.

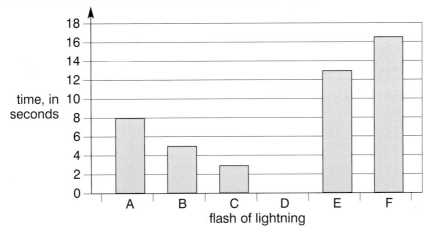

(i) On the bar chart, draw a bar for flash D. Use a ruler.   *1 mark*

(ii) Which flash of lightning was closest to Omar?
Give the correct letter.

--   *1 mark*

(iii) Describe how the distance between the storm and Omar changed as the
storm moved between flash A and flash F.

---   *1 mark*

Maximum 4 marks

10 Ruth is investigating how much a piece of wood can bend. She hangs some
masses on the end of the piece of wood and measures how far the wood has bent.

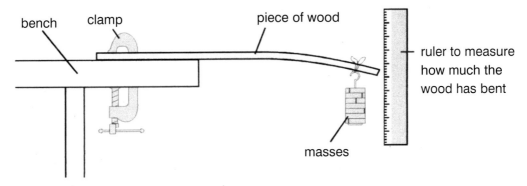

(a) Give the name of the force which pulls the masses downwards.

---   *1 mark*

(b)   The graph below shows Ruth's results.

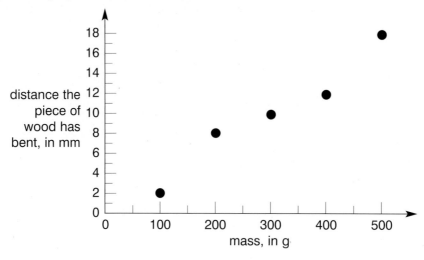

(i)   Complete the graph by drawing a straight line of best fit.

1 mark

(ii)   A mass of 350 g is hung on the piece of wood. How much does the wood bend?

_____ mm

1 mark

Maximum 3 marks

THIS IS THE START OF THE TIER 5–7 PAPER

11   The diagram shows an oak tree.

(a)   An oak tree takes in water and oxygen from the soil.
      Name **one** other **type** of substance an oak tree needs to take in from
      the soil.

      -- *1 mark*

(b)   The roots of an oak tree are long and split into many smaller roots.
      How does this help the tree to absorb water?

      -- *1 mark*

(c)   By the time winter comes, the oak tree has lost its leaves. Explain
      why this stops the growth of an oak tree.

      -- *1 mark*

(d)   The drawing shows a caterpillar of a moth called the Oak Beauty.
      These caterpillars feed on oak leaves and woodland birds eat them.

caterpillar

twig

Describe how the appearance of the caterpillar can help it to survive.

-- *2 marks*

Maximum 5 marks

12 (a) Drinking large amounts of alcohol every day can damage the liver. The type of damage is called cirrhosis, and it can kill a person quickly. The graph below shows the number of people dying from cirrhosis of the liver, in Paris, between 1935 and 1965.

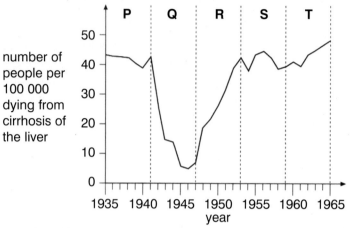

During which period of time, P, Q, R, S or T, was it difficult to get alcohol?

----

1 mark

(b) Alcohol is a drug. Which property makes alcohol a drug? Tick the correct box.

It is soluble in water. ☐   It can provide energy. ☐

It is a chemical. ☐   It affects the nervous system. ☐

1 mark

(c) Look at the graph on the right.

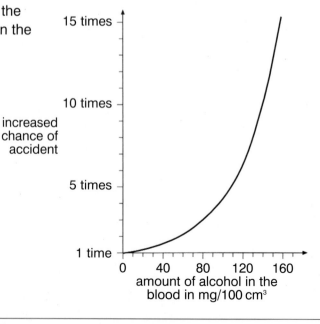

(i)   Using the graph, describe how increasing the amount of alcohol in the blood affects the chance of having an accident.

--- *2 marks*

(ii) Which of the following statements could be used to explain why alcohol in the blood could cause accidents?
Tick the correct box.

Alcohol cools the body. ☐

Alcohol increases the time a person takes to react. ☐

Alcohol is a stimulant. ☐

Alcohol makes a person happy. ☐

1 mark

Maximum 5 marks

13 The drawings show some plant and animal cells. Each cell has a different function.

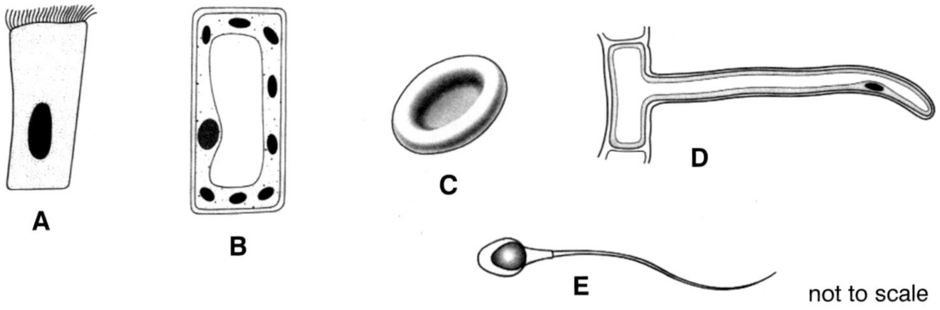

A   B   C   D   E   not to scale

(a)   Give the name of cell C.

--- *1 mark*

(b)   The main functions of two of the cells are listed below.
Write the letter of the correct cell next to each function.

(i)   photosynthesis ---

(ii) the movement of mucus --- *2 marks*

(c) (i) Give the name of the organ where cell E is produced.

----
1 mark

(ii) Give the name of the part of a plant where cell B is found.

----
1 mark

Maximum 5 marks

14 Some roads are made of concrete. The concrete is laid in sections with small gaps between them.

concrete section
gap
concrete section

(a) (i) What happens to the size of most objects when they get hotter?

----
1 mark

(ii) When the temperature rises, what will happen to the gaps between the concrete sections?

----
1 mark

(iii) When the temperature rises, what might happen to the sections of concrete if there are **no** gaps between them?

----
1 mark

(b) The gaps between the concrete sections are filled with tar. The tar becomes soft when it is warm.
Why is it important that the tar becomes soft?

----
1 mark

Maximum 4 marks

15 (a) Sunil picked yellow, red and purple primula flowers from his garden.

He dipped the different flower petals into water and into two different solutions.
The pH of one solution was 1 and the pH of the other was 10.
The table shows the results.

colour of flower petals	in solutions of pH 1	in water pH 7	in solution of pH 10
yellow	stayed yellow	stayed yellow	stayed yellow
red	stayed red	stayed red	turned green
purple	turned pink	stayed purple	turned blue

Which colour of flower petal would be most useful to make an indicator for
both acids **and** alkalis? Explain your answer.

--- *2 marks*

Sunil crushed petals from each flower separately in some liquid and poured
off the coloured solutions. Then he put drops of each coloured solution into
the middle of different pieces of filter paper.

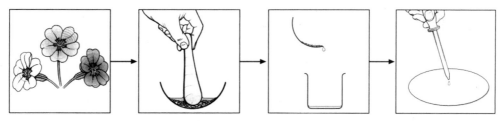

The solutions spread out on the filter paper. The diagrams show his results.

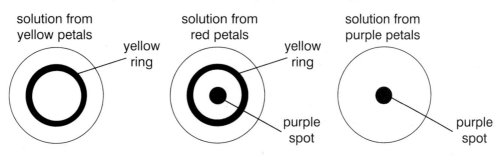

(b) What is the name of this method of investigating coloured substances?

--- *1 mark*

(c)   Sunil made notes on his experiment. Some words are missing.
Complete the sentences.

> When I crushed a flower in a liquid it produced a coloured solution. This is
>
> because a coloured substance had .... in the liquid.
>
> This shows that the liquid is a .... for these
>
> coloured substances.
>
> My experiment shows that one of the flowers probably contained two
>
> coloured substances. This was the .... flower.

3 marks

Maximum 6 marks

16   The table shows the time taken for the Earth, Mars and Venus to orbit the Sun.

planet	time taken to orbit the Sun, in Earth years
Earth	1.0
Mars	1.9
Venus	0.6

The diagram shows the orbits of the Earth, Mars and Venus round the Sun, at one particular time. The arrows show the direction in which the planets move.

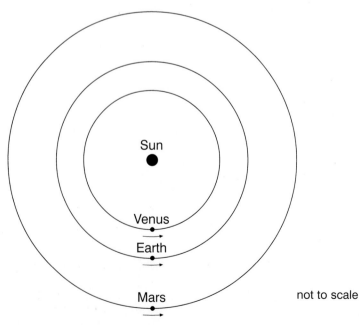

At the time shown in the diagram, the three planets were lined up with the Sun.

(a)   Show the position of the Earth **three** months after the planets were lined up, by marking a point on the Earth's orbit.
Label the point E.

1 mark

(b)   (i)   Show the approximate position of Mars **three** Earth months after the planets were lined up, by marking a point on Mars's orbit.
Label the point M.

1 mark

(ii)   Explain why Mars is in this position.

----
1 mark

(c)   (i)   Show the approximate position of Venus **three** Earth months after the planets were lined up, by marking a point on Venus's orbit.
Label the point V.

1 mark

(ii)   Explain why Venus is in this position.

----
1 mark

Maximum 5 marks

17   Sarah made a cotton reel vehicle like the one shown in the diagram.
The pencil is wound round and round so that it winds up the rubber band.
A piece of candle wax next to the cotton reel lets the rubber band slowly unwind.

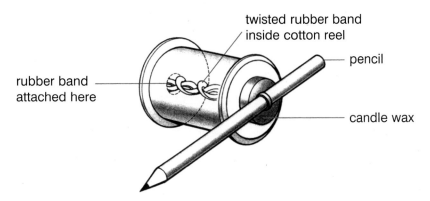

twisted rubber band
inside cotton reel

pencil

rubber band
attached here

candle wax

(a)   As the rubber band unwinds, the candle wax slips and the cotton reel turns.
Name the force which acts between the cotton reel and the candle wax.

----
1 mark

(b)   Sarah tested the vehicle by letting it run along a horizontal table top.

    (i)   She noticed that the vehicle gradually slowed down.
             Give the reason for this.

            -- *1 mark*

    (ii)   Describe what Sarah could do to make the rubber band move this
             vehicle faster.

            -- *1 mark*

Maximum 3 marks

18   Joe saw two
types of swing
in the park.

He noticed that the time for one complete swing, forward and back, was different
for the two types of swing.

He did **not** know whether the length of the chains or the mass of the person
affected the time for one complete swing.

He made model swings
and measured how long
it took for 10 complete
swings in 4 investigations.

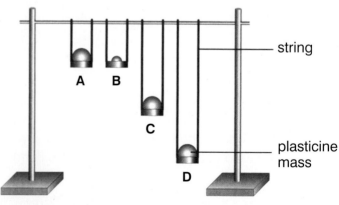

Here are his results.

	investigation			
	A	**B**	**C**	**D**
length of string, in cm	25	25	50	75
mass of plasticine, in g	100	50	100	100
time for 10 complete swings, in s	10.0	10.0	14.2	17.4

Here is Joe's conclusion:

Changing the mass of plasticine has no effect on the time taken for 10 complete swings.

(a)   Which **two** of his investigations, A, B, C or D, provided evidence to support his conclusion?

_____ and _____   *1 mark*

(b)   Look at the results table.
   (i)   Describe how the length of the string affects the time for 10 complete swings.

   _____

   _____   *1 mark*

   (ii)   Which **three** of his investigations are best evidence for this?

   _____ and _____ and _____   *1 mark*

(c)   Use his previous table of results to predict the times for 10 complete swings in two further investigations E and F.
Write your answers in the table below.

	investigation	
	E	**F**
length of string, in cm	25	100
mass of plasticine, in g	25	100
time for 10 complete swings, in s	------------------	------------------

1 mark

Maximum 4 marks

THIS IS THE END OF THE TIER 3–6 PAPER

19 When white light is shone through a glass prism the light bends and splits into the colours of the spectrum.

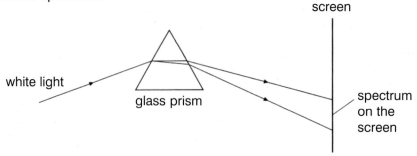

(a) (i) What word describes the bending of light as it enters and leaves glass?

--- *1 mark*

(ii) What word describes the splitting of light into the colours of the spectrum?

--- *1 mark*

(b) Some leaves from a buttercup plant were ground up in a solvent and filtered to give a green solution of chlorophyll. A glass container of this green solution was put in the rays of coloured light.

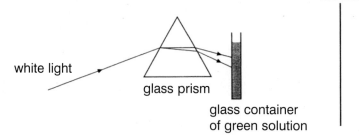

What change in the spectrum would you see on the screen?
Explain your answer.

--- *2 marks*

(c) Why is it necessary to grind up the buttercup leaves to release the chlorophyll from the cells?

--- *1 mark*

(d) Buttercup plants grow mainly in open fields. Dog's Mercury is a plant which grows mainly in woodland. The graph shows how the rate of photosynthesis in these two plants changes as the light intensity changes.

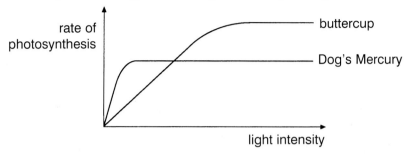

Why do Dog's Mercury plants grow better than buttercups in woodland? Use the graph to help you.

--- *1 mark*

Maximum 6 marks

20 The diagram shows two types of cell in the lining of the windpipe.

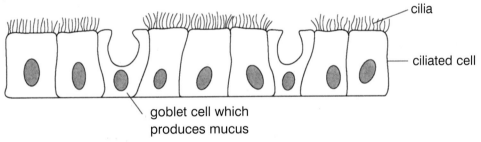

(a) (i) These cells work together to keep the lungs free of bacteria and dust particles.
What word describes a group of similar cells which work together?

--- *1 mark*

(ii) Mucus is a sticky substance.
Describe how **mucus** and **cilia** keep the lungs free of bacteria and dust particles.

--- *2 marks*

(b)   When a person breathes in cigarette smoke, the goblet cells produce extra
      mucus and the cilia are damaged.
      What will be the consequences of this?

      --- *2 marks*

(c)   Give the names of **two** harmful substances in cigarette smoke. In what way is
      each one harmful?

      1   name of substance --

          harmful effect --

          ----

      2   name of substance --

          harmful effect --

      --- *2 marks*

                                                                             Maximum 7 marks

21   The diagrams represent the arrangement of atoms or molecules in four different
         substances, A, B, C, and D.

      A   B   C   D

                                                              not to scale

Each of the circles, ○, ◐ and ●, represents an atom of a different element.

(a)   (i)   Which substance is a compound?

            --   *1 mark*

      (ii) Which substance is a mixture?

            --   *1 mark*

(iii)   Which **two** substances are elements?

-------------------------------- and --------------------------------   *1 mark*

(iv)   Which **two** substances could be good thermal conductors?

-------------------------------- and --------------------------------   *1 mark*

(v)   Which substance could be carbon dioxide?

--   *1 mark*

(b)   The following experiment was set up. Test-tubes containing substances B and C were placed together as shown. The substances did **not** react. They were left for five minutes.

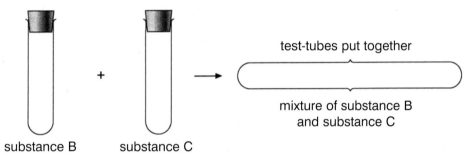

(i)   How many molecules are there in the mixture compared to the total number in substances B and C?

-- *1 mark*

(ii)   Complete the diagram which is a model of this experiment.   *1 mark*

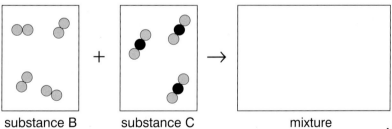

substance B   substance C   mixture

Maximum 7 marks

22   Railway lines can be joined together by pouring molten iron into the gap between them.

(a)   The molten iron is produced by the reaction between powdered aluminium and iron oxide.
Complete the word equation for the reaction.

aluminium + iron oxide → iron + ---   *1 mark*

(b) Iron can be produced from a mixture of aluminium and iron oxide but **not** from a mixture of copper and iron oxide.
Write the names of the **three** metals, in the order of their reactivity.

most reactive ....

....

....   *1 mark*

(c) The list shows the names and symbols of five metals in order of their reactivity.

name	symbol
sodium	Na
calcium	Ca
magnesium	Mg
zinc	Zn
silver	Ag

(i) What, if anything, would be the result of heating zinc powder with calcium oxide?

.... *1 mark*

(ii) Write down the **name** of a metal in the list that will **not** react with a solution of magnesium sulphate.

....   *1 mark*

(d) The powdered metal with the symbol Zn burns in air.
Write the **word equation** for the reaction.

.... *2 marks*

Maximum 6 marks

23 A video recorder is loaded with a tape which plays for 180 minutes.
The length of the tape is 260 m.

(a) (i) Calculate the speed of the tape, in metres per minute.

.... m/min   *1 mark*

(ii) What is the speed of the tape in metres per second?

.... m/s   *1 mark*

(b)   To rewind the tape quickly, a different motor is used which rewinds the tape at a maximum speed of 1.08 m/s.

    (i)   At this speed, how long would it take to rewind the tape completely? Give the units.

--- *1 mark*

    (ii) In fact, it takes slightly longer than this to rewind the tape. Explain why.

--- *1 mark*

Maximum 4 marks

24 Karen wants to pump up her car tyre.
Her pump has a piston with an area of 7 cm².

175 N

area = 7 cm²

Karen pushes the handle down with a force of 175 N.

(a)   What pressure does she exert on the air in the pump?

-- N/cm?   *1 mark*

(b)   The air pressure in the tyre is 27 N/cm².
What pressure would be needed **in the pump** in order to pump more air into the tyre?

--- *1 mark*

(c)   Another of Karen's car tyres exerts a pressure of 30 N/cm² on the road.
The area of the tyre in contact with the road is 95 cm².
What is the force exerted by the tyre on the road?

--- N   *1 mark*

Maximum 3 marks

THIS IS THE END OF THE TIER 5–7 PAPER

Paper 2

THIS IS THE START OF THE TIER 3–6 PAPER

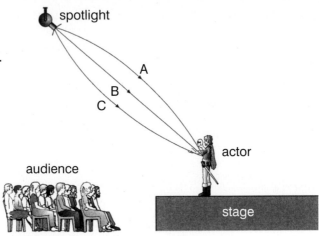

spotlight

1 An actor is on a stage in a theatre. A spotlight is shining on him.

A

B

C

actor

audience

stage

(a)   A ray of light travels from the spotlight to the actor.

(i)   Which line shows the ray? Give the correct letter. ....   *1 mark*

(ii) How long does the light take to travel from the spotlight to the actor? Tick the correct box.

about a hundred millionth of a second   ☐

about a tenth of a second   ☐

about a second   ☐

about ten seconds   ☐

1 mark

(b)   The actor's voice sounds different to the people in the front and back rows of the audience.

(i)   How does the actor's voice sound different to a person in the back row?

....

....   *1 mark*

(ii) Complete the sentence with **longer**, **shorter**, or **exactly the same**.

When the actor is at the back of the stage, the time his voice takes to

reach the audience is ....   *1 mark*

Maximum 4 marks

2   Ali made a cat-flap to fit in a door.

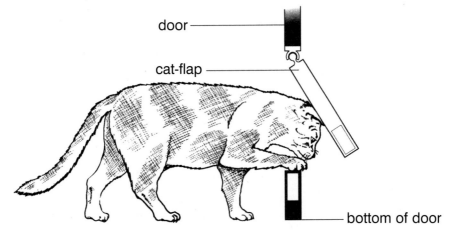

door

cat-flap

bottom of door

(a)   (i)   On the diagram above, draw an arrow to show the direction of the force of the cat's head on the cat-flap.   *1 mark*

     (ii)   Add a label to the diagram to show the pivot of the cat-flap. Label it P.   *1 mark*

When the cat has gone through the cat-flap, the weight of the cat-flap makes the flap close.

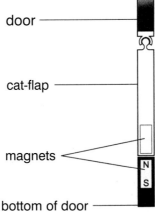

door

cat-flap

magnets

bottom of door

(b)   Ali used two bar magnets to keep the cat-flap closed, so that it does **not** blow open in the wind.

On the diagram above, label **both** the North and South poles on the magnet in the cat-flap.   *1 mark*

(c)   Friction at the pivot made the cat-flap squeak. What could Ali put on the pivot to make the friction less?

----

1 mark

Maximum 4 marks

3 Sound levels are measured in decibels (dB).
The graph shows the recommended maximum times people should listen to sounds of different levels.
At longer times there could be serious damage to hearing.

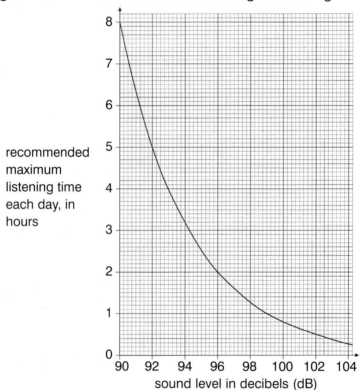

recommended maximum listening time each day, in hours

sound level in decibels (dB)

(a) What is the maximum time each day for listening to a personal stereo at 96 dB?

.... hours

1 mark

(b) In what way could a sound of more than 120 dB damage the ear?

....

1 mark

(a) (i) Sally works for five hours in a nightclub. What should the maximum sound level be in the nightclub so that her hearing is **not** damaged?
Use the graph to find your answer.

.... dB

1 mark

(ii) How can ear plugs protect Sally's ears?

....

....

1 mark

Maximum 4 marks

4 Alan and Aysha saw a poster claiming that Glossy washing-up liquid makes more bubbles than other washing-up liquids.

They investigated the amount of bubbles three different washing-up liquids made.

They added each type of washing-up liquid to water in a test-tube and shook it.

(a) What would they see if the results of their test supported the claim made on the poster?

-- *1 mark*

(b) Why should they use the same volume of washing-up liquid in each test-tube?

-- *1 mark*

(c) The first time they tried this investigation **all** the washing-up liquids made bubbles which went to the tops of the test-tubes.
Why was this a problem?

-- *1 mark*

(d)   Jane tried the investigation again using less washing-up liquid in each test-tube.
       She made a prediction about Shine washing-up liquid.
       The photograph shows her results.

Glossy   Shine   Fresh

Jane's results support her prediction about Shine.

What was Jane's prediction?

--- *1 mark*

Maximum 4 marks

5   Water from red cabbage can be used to find out if a liquid is acidic, alkaline
        or neutral.

type of liquid added to the cabbage water	colour of the cabbage water
acidic	red
alkaline	blue
neutral	purple

John added three different liquids to the cabbage water.

(a)   Use the information above to complete the table below.   *3 marks*

liquid added to the cabbage water	colour of the cabbage water	is the liquid acidic, alkaline or neutral?
water	purple	
lemon juice		acidic
washing-up liquid	blue	

(b)   What word describes chemicals which change colour in acids or alkalis?
        Tick the correct box.

filters ☐   indicators ☐

liquids ☐   solids ☐

1 mark

Maximum 4 marks

6   A Japanese volcano erupted in 1936. Molten sulphur poured out of the volcano.
        When it cooled it formed rock sulphur.

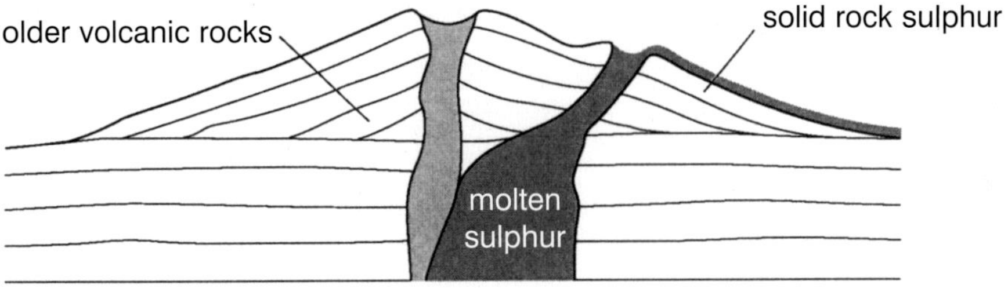

(a)   (i)   Which word describes molten rock that is underground?
                Choose from **lava** or **magma** or **oil**.

        ----
        1 mark

        (ii)   Which type of rock do volcanoes produce?
                Choose from **igneous** or **metamorphic** or **sedimentary**.

        ----
        1 mark

(b)   Sulphur is a **non**-metallic element. It is yellow and melts at 115°C.
        Complete the sentences about sulphur.

        (i)   Sulphur is a poor conductor of

        ----
        1 mark

        (ii)   At 115°C sulphur changes from

                a ----------------------------- into a ----------------------------- *2 marks*

(c)   Sulphur burns in air to form an oxide.
        What gas in the air reacts with sulphur when it burns?

        ----
        1 mark

        Maximum 6 marks

7 Gravy powder contains:

- a brown substance to make the gravy brown;
- cornflour to make the gravy thick.

Dan mixed some gravy powder with cold water in a beaker.
An hour later, the contents of the beaker looked like this:

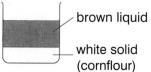

brown liquid

white solid
(cornflour)

(a) Use the words in the list below to fill the gaps in the following sentences.

solvent   solution   soluble   insoluble

The brown substance dissolves in water to form a

brown ....

The cornflour settles at the bottom of the beaker because

it is .... in water.

Water is the .... in this experiment.   *3 marks*

(b) Dan wanted to separate the brown liquid from the white solid.
What could he do to separate them?

....   *1 mark*

(c) Dan put a little of the brown liquid in a dish. The next day there was only a
brown solid left in the dish. What had happened to the water?

....

....   *1 mark*

(d) Dan wanted to get pure water from the rest of the brown liquid.
He set up the apparatus shown below.

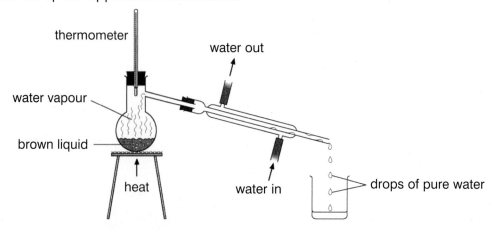

Water vapour from the brown liquid changed into drops of pure water which were collected in the beaker. What process caused the drops of water to form from the vapour? Tick the correct box.

boiling ☐   condensing ☐

dissolving ☐   melting ☐

1 mark

Maximum 6 marks

8 (a) Alex poured some pond water into three beakers. She then put waterweed into each beaker. She put the beakers in different places.

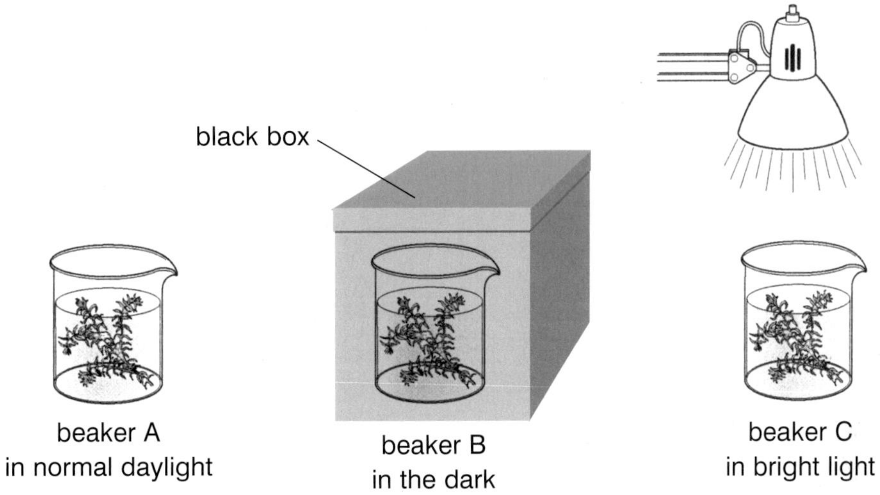

black box

beaker A
in normal daylight

beaker B
in the dark

beaker C
in bright light

(i) In which beaker did the waterweed grow best? Give the correct letter.

-------------------------------   *1 mark*

(ii) The waterweed in the box changed from dark green to pale yellow. Why did this happen?

-- *1 mark*

(b) In the school pond there were lots of water lilies with large leaves covering the surface.
There were **not** many plants growing below the surface.
Suggest a reason for this.

-- *1 mark*

(c)　In another experiment, Alex put similar pieces of waterweed into two more beakers of pond water.
She added fertiliser to one of them.
She kept them both by a window.

beaker D
containing
waterweed
and pond water

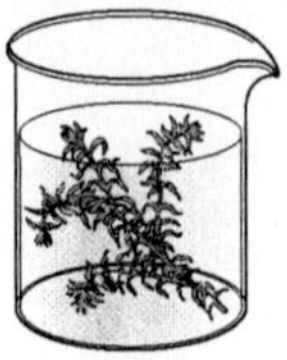

beaker E
containing
waterweed and
pond water
plus fertiliser

(i)　Alex added fertiliser to beaker E. Suggest the results of this experiment.

-- *1 mark*

(ii)　What do fertilisers contain to help plants grow?
Tick the correct box.

fat ☐　　　minerals ☐

sand ☐　　　sugar ☐ *1 mark*

Maximum 5 marks

9　Each of the animals in the drawings below belongs to a different group.

(a)　One the line beneath each drawing, write the name of the group the animal belongs to.
Choose names from the list below.

amphibians　crustaceans　insects　mammals　molluscs　reptiles

------------------　------------------　------------------　------------------
　　A　　　　　　　**B**　　　　　　　**C**　　　　　　　**D**
4 marks

(b)　Which of the animals drawn above are invertebrates?
Give the correct letters.

------------------ and ------------------ *2 marks*

Maximum 6 marks

THIS IS THE START OF THE TIER 5–7 PAPER

10   The picture shows a man called Aristotle. He lived in Greece over 2000 years ago.

Aristotle said that the heavier an object is, the faster it will fall to the ground.

(a)   The drawings below show a bowling ball, a cricket ball and a ping-pong ball.
Lila dropped them all at the same time from the same height.

bowling ball   cricket ball   ping-pong ball
mass = 5000 g   mass = 160 g   mass = 2.5 g

If Aristotle was correct, which of the three balls would you expect to reach the
ground first? Give the reason for your answer.

....

....   *1 mark*

(b)   Joe said that it would be a fairer test if Lila had only used a cricket ball and a
hollow plastic ball as shown below.

cricket ball   hollow plastic ball
mass = 160 g   mass = 56 g

Why was Joe correct?

....

....   *1 mark*

(c) About 400 years ago in Italy, a man called Galileo had a different idea. He said that all objects dropped from the same height would reach the ground at the same time.

(i) Lila dropped a hammer and a feather at the same time from the same height.

If Galileo was correct, which, if either, would reach the ground first?

-- *1 mark*

(ii) Gravity acts on both the hammer and the feather as they fall.
Give the name of **one** other force which acts on them as they fall.

-- *1 mark*

(iii) An astronaut on the Moon dropped a hammer and a feather at the same time from the same height.

How would the results of the astronaut's experiment on the Moon be different from Lila's experiment on the Earth?

Explain your answer.

-- *2 marks*

Maximum 6 marks

11 The diagram shows two dodgem cars at a fairground. The circuit symbols for the motor and pedal for each dodgem car are shown on the diagram.

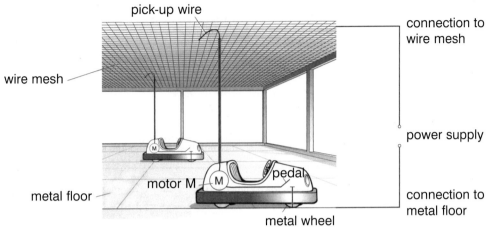

pick-up wire

connection to wire mesh

wire mesh

power supply

motor M

pedal

metal floor

connection to metal floor

metal wheel

(a) Complete the following sentence:

Each dodgem car is connected to the power supply through the

.... which is in contact with

the wire mesh, and through the ....

which is in contact with the metal floor.   *1 mark*

(b) Dodgem cars are connected using parallel circuits.
Complete the circuit diagram below for the **two** dodgem cars.

Use **two** motor symbols, ⎯(M)⎯ , and **two** switch symbols, ⎯╱⎯ .

The power supply for the circuit has been drawn for you.

connection to wire mesh

power supply

connection to metal floor   *2 marks*

(c) Even when the power supply is switched on, the dodgem car will **not** move until the pedal is pressed. Give the reason for this.

....

....   *1 mark*

(d) A man looks after the dodgem cars during the rides.
     Why does the man **not** get an electric shock as he walks across the metal floor?

     -- *1 mark*

(e) During one ride, the two dodgem cars are running. The pick-up wire on one car snaps off. Describe how this affects:

     (i)   the dodgem car with the broken pick-up wire;

           -- *1 mark*

     (ii) the other dodgem car.

           -- *1 mark*

                                                               Maximum 7 marks

12 Bees and wasps are both insects which use a sting as part of their defence.
     The pH values of their stings are shown on the diagrams.

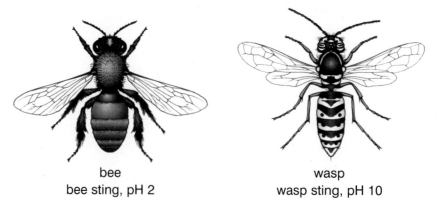

bee
bee sting, pH 2

wasp
wasp sting, pH 10

(a) Complete the table below to show whether the stings are acidic or alkaline and what colour they would turn universal indicator paper.

	acidic or alkaline	colour of universal indicator paper
bee sting (pH 2)		
wasp sting (pH 10)		

                                                                         2 marks

(b)   The table below shows five household substances and the pH of each substance.

name of substance	pH of substance
bicarbonate toothpaste	8
lemon juice	3
vinegar	4
washing soda	11
water	7

Give the name of **one** substance in the table which would neutralise each sting.

(i)   bee sting .... *1 mark*

(ii) wasp sting .... *1 mark*

Maximum 4 marks

13   Sailors used to suffer from an illness called scurvy caused by a poor diet on long journeys.
James Lind was a doctor who tested treatments for scurvy. He predicted that **all acids cure scurvy**.

I think that all acids will cure scurvy.

He gave six pairs of sailors with scurvy exactly the same meals but he also gave each pair a different addition to their diet.

pair of sailors	addition to their diet	effect after one week
1	some apple cider	beginning to recover
2	25 drops of very dilute sulphuric acid to gargle with *	still had scurvy
3	2 teaspoons of vinegar	still had scurvy
4	half a pint of sea water *	still had scurvy
5	2 oranges and 1 lemon	recovered
6	herbs and spices and acidified barley water	still had scurvy

* DANGER! DO NOT TRY THIS.

(a) Does the evidence in the table support the prediction that all acids cure scurvy?
Tick the correct box.

☐   ☐

    yes   no

Use the table to explain your answer.

-- *1 mark*

(b) (i) Give the **one** factor James Lind **changed** in this experiment.
(This is called the independent variable.)

-- *1 mark*

(ii) Give the factor James Lind **examined** in this experiment.
(This is called the dependent variable.)

-- *1 mark*

(c)   James Lind's evidence suggested that oranges and lemons cured scurvy. At a later time, other scientists did the following:

●   They separated citric acid from the fruit.

●   They predicted that citric acid would cure scurvy.

●   They tested their prediction by giving pure citric acid as an addition to the diet of sailors with scurvy.

●   They found it did **not** cure scurvy.

The scientists had to make a different prediction.

Suggest a new prediction about a cure for scurvy that is consistent with the evidence collected.

--- *1 mark*

(d)   Explain why it is necessary to investigate the effects of changes in diet over a period of more than one week.

--- *1 mark*

Maximum 5 marks

14   (a)   George used the apparatus below to find out what substances are produced when methanol burns.

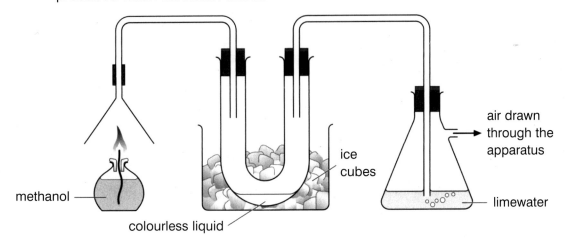

As the methanol burned, two different gases were produced.

(i)   One of these gases condensed in the U-Tube to give a colourless
       liquid.
       Give the name of this liquid.

       ---   *1 mark*

(ii)   The other gas turned the limewater cloudy.
       Give the name of this gas.

       ---   *1 mark*

(b)   Methanol is sometimes used in antifreeze. It can be added to water in
       car windscreen wash-bottles to prevent the water from freezing in cold
       conditions.

(i)   The label on the bottle of antifreeze has two hazard warning symbols.
       What **two** precautions would you need to take when using this
       antifreeze?

       1 ---

          ----

       2 ---

          ---   *1 mark*

(ii) Water freezes at 0°C. The label on the bottle shows how the freezing point changes when different amounts of antifreeze are added to water.

Terry put a mixture containing 10% antifreeze into the wash-bottle of his car. During the night the temperature dropped to -14°C.
The wash-bottle burst.
Explain why the wash-bottle burst.

-- *2 marks*

Maximum 5 marks

15 Sarah and Jim investigated the effect of temperature on the solubility of copper sulphate.

They dissolved copper sulphate crystals in the same volume of water until no more would dissolve. This means the solution was saturated.
They measured the mass of copper sulphate needed to make a saturated solution using water at different temperatures.

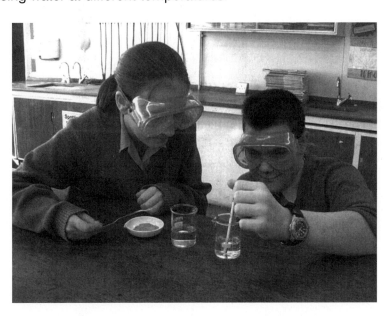

They plotted their results on a grid.

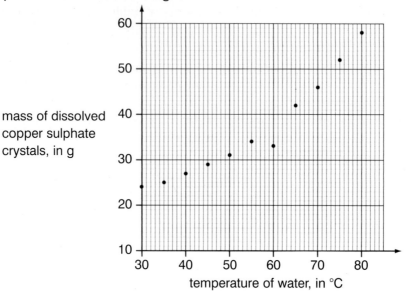

mass of dissolved copper sulphate crystals, in g

temperature of water, in °C

(a) (i) One of the mass readings appears to be wrong (anomalous). Circle the anomalous result on the graph. *1 mark*

(ii) Draw a smooth curve of best fit on the graph. *1 mark*

(iii) Use the graph to predict a more likely measurement of mass for the anomalous result.

----------------------- g *1 mark*

(b) Suggest **one** mistake Sarah and Jim might have made to produce this anomalous result.

--- *1 mark*

Maximum 4 marks

16 Diagram 1 below shows the lungs and the trachea, the airway leading to the lungs. One of the lungs is drawn in section.

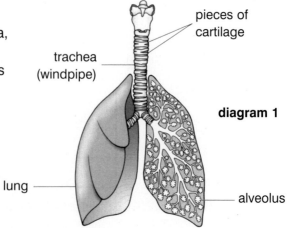

pieces of cartilage

trachea (windpipe)

diagram 1

lung

alveolus

(a)   In the wall of the trachea, there are pieces of a stiff material called cartilage.
      Why is this stiff material necessary in the wall of the trachea?

      ---   *1 mark*

(b)   Diagram 2 below shows one alveolus and its blood supply.

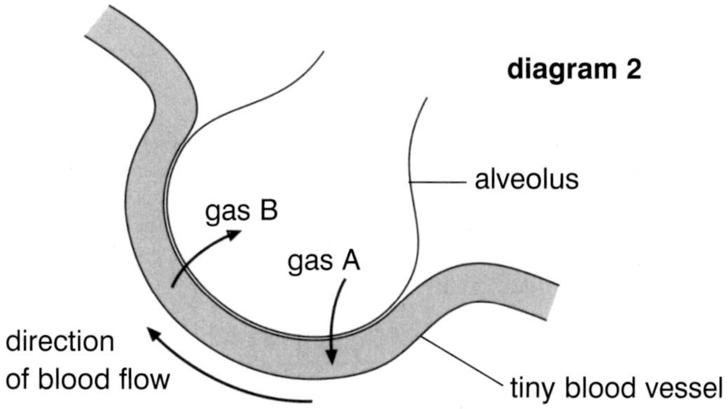

diagram 2

alveolus

gas B

gas A

direction
of blood flow

tiny blood vessel

   (i)   Look at diagram 2.
         Gas A **enters** the blood from the alveolus.
         Gas B **leaves** the blood and enters the alveolus.
         What are the names of gases A and B?

         gas A ---

         gas B ---   *1 mark*

   (ii) Give **one** reason why it is easy for gases to pass across the wall of
         an alveolus.

         --   *1 mark*

(c)   This diagram   cilia
      shows a ciliated cell
      from the lining of
      the airway.

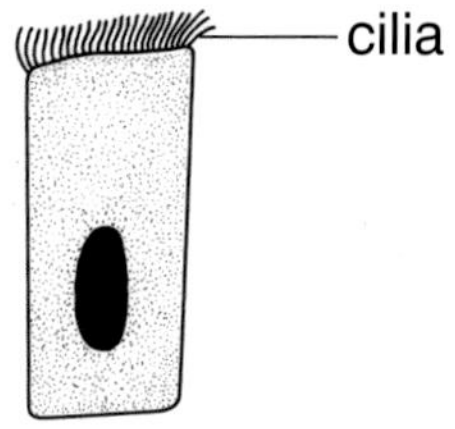

   (i)   What is the function of this cell in the airway?

         --   *1 mark*

(ii)   This cell is affected by substances in cigarette smoke.
       What effect does cigarette smoke have on the cilia?

       ....

       ....   *1 mark*

(iii) Give the name of the substance, in cigarette smoke, which causes
       addiction to smoking.

       ....   *1 mark*

                                                                    Maximum 6 marks

17   (a)   Over many years, cliffs may be affected by weathering.
              Describe one effect of weathering on a cliff.

              ....

              ....   *1 mark*

        (b)   The photograph shows a piece of sandstone.

              (i)   The sandstone in the photograph contains a fossil.
                     What is a fossil?

                     ....

                     ....   *1 mark*

              (ii)   What group of rocks does sandstone belong to?

                     ....   *1 mark*

(c) Granite and basalt are igneous rocks. They contain crystals but **no** fossils.

   (i) How are igneous rocks formed?

   --- *1 mark*

   (ii) Explain why igneous rocks do **not** contain fossils.

   --- *1 mark*

   (iii) Granite takes much longer to form than basalt.
         How will the size of the crystals in granite be different from the size of
         the crystals in basalt?

   --- *1 mark*

                                                              Maximum 6 marks

18 A teacher set up the following apparatus behind a safety screen.
She placed 1 g of icing sugar in the end of the rubber tubing inside the tin, as
shown below.

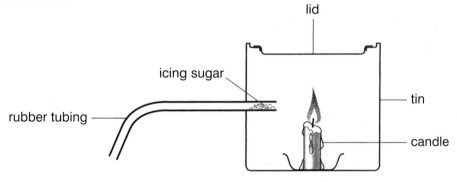

The teacher blew through the other end of the rubber tubing.
The icing sugar came into contact with the flame.
There was a loud explosion and the lid was blown off the tin.

(a) Complete the following sentence describing the energy changes which took
     place.

     -------------------------------- energy in the icing sugar changed to

     -------------------------------- energy and -------------------------------- energy.   *3 marks*

(b)   As a result of the explosion, the lid of the tin was pushed off.
      Explain what had happened to the gas molecules inside the tin to make
      this happen.

      ---   *2 marks*

(c)   When icing sugar is burned in this experiment, the gas **used** and the gas
      produced are the same as when energy is released from sugar in the cells of
      the body.

      (i)   Which gas, in the air, is **used** when the icing sugar burns?

            ---   *1 mark*

      (ii) Give the name of the gas **produced** when the icing sugar burns.

            ---   *1 mark*

(d)   The table below shows the energy values of four food substances.

food substance	energy value, in kJ per 100 g
icing sugar	1680
curry powder	979
flour	1450
custard powder	630

      The teacher repeated the experiment with 1 g of custard powder.
      What difference would this make to the experiment?

      ---   *1 mark*

                                                                          Maximum 8 marks

 THIS IS THE END OF THE TIER 3–6 PAPER

19 Peter measured the current through each of three similar bulbs in a parallel circuit.

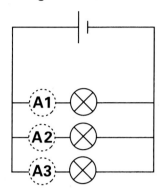

He had only one ammeter and he placed it first at **A1**, then **A2**, then **A3**, in order to measure the currents.

The table shows his results.

position of ammeter	current, in amps
A1	0.14
A2	0.16
A3	0.15

(a) He expected the current readings to be the **same** for each bulb but found they were **different**.
Suggest **two** reasons why the readings were different.

1 ....

2 .... *2 marks*

(b) Peter then measured the current at **A4** and recorded it as 0.45 A.
He concluded that the current at **A4** could be calculated by adding together the currents through each of the bulbs at positions **A1**, **A2** and **A3**.

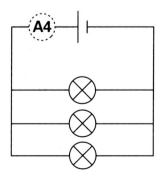

He added two more similar bulbs to his circuit, in parallel.
The current through each bulb was 0.15 A.
Use Peter's conclusion to predict the current at **A4** with the 5 bulbs in
the circuit.

-------------------------- A

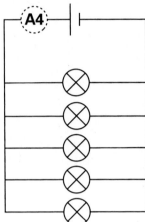

1 mark

(c)   Peter left the circuit connected overnight. He used a datalogger to measure
the current at position **A4** at regular intervals of time. The next morning the
bulbs were dim.

Using the axes below, sketch (do **not** plot) how the current at position **A4**
might change with time.

Indicate on the graph:

(i)   The correct labels for each axis, including the correct units.

(ii)   The shape of the graph you would expect to obtain.

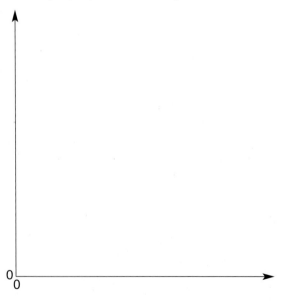

2 marks

Maximum 5 marks

20 (a) Peter tried to obtain a mixture of red and green light.
He used white light from a spotlight and slotted a red filter and a green filter in front of it as shown below.

red and green
filters slot in here

The diagram below represents Peter's experiment.

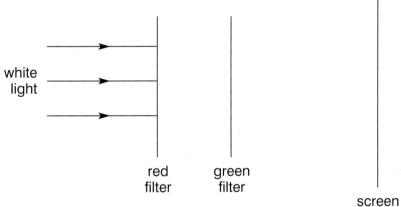

white
light

red   green
filter   filter

screen

(i) **No** light reached the screen. Explain why.

--- *2 marks*

(ii) Peter cut a circular hole in the green filter.
Describe what Peter would see on the screen.

--- *1 mark*

(b)   Peter used two spotlights to shine a mixture of red and green light on to some red curtains.

   (i)   What colour did the red curtains appear in this light?

   .... *1 mark*

   (ii) Give the reasons why they appeared this colour.

   ....

   ....

   ....

   .... *2 marks*

Maximum 6 marks

21   A headline from a newspaper is shown below.

British Power Stations cause Acid Rain in Scandinavia

Some countries claim that acid rain caused by power stations in Britain damages their forests.

Others argue that coal-burning power stations produce cheap electricity and that plants can stand some level of acid rain.

Imagine you are planning a laboratory investigation of the claim:

'plants can stand some level of acid rain'.

Assume you have access to whatever laboratory equipment you need, including:
   ● seeds
   ● acid
   ● seed trays
   ● soil

Plan a laboratory investigation to test the claim that **'plants can stand some level of acid rain'.**

(a)   Name a factor you would need to vary in your investigation.
        (This is the independent variable.)

--   *1 mark*

(b)   (i)   What factor would you examine to see the effect?
                (This is the dependent variable.)

--   *1 mark*

        (ii)   How could you measure this dependent variable?

--   *1 mark*

(c)   Suggest **one** factor you would control to ensure that your
        investigation is fair.

--   *1 mark*

Maximum 4 marks

22   In 1610, the Italian scientist, Galileo, observed four bright moons near
        Jupiter. Each night the moons moved.

(a)   (i)   The Sun and stars are light sources, and the planets are seen
                by reflected light. Explain how we can see the moons of Jupiter.

--   *2 marks*

        (ii)   The four moons are approximately the same distance from
                the Earth.
                However, they do **not** have the same brightness.
                Suggest **one** reason for this.

--   *1 mark*

(b) The table shows the distances of the four moons from the centre of Jupiter, and the times of their orbits. Europa's distance has been left out.

name of moon	distance from Jupiter, in millions of km	time for one orbit, in earth days
Io	0.42	1.8
Europa		3.6
Ganymede	1.07	7.2
Callisto	1.88	16.7

The graph was plotted using the information in the table.

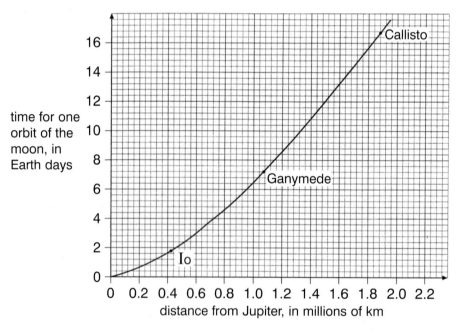

Use the graph to estimate Europa's distance from Jupiter.

.... millions of km   *1 mark*

(c) Galileo realised that Jupiter and its moons formed a model of our Solar System. In this model:

what did Jupiter represent? ....

what did the moons represent? .... *1 mark*

Maximum 5 marks

23 Aisha placed small samples of four different metals on a spotting tile.
She added drops of copper sulphate solution to each metal.

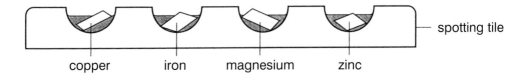

copper   iron   magnesium   zinc

Aisha repeated the experiment with fresh samples of the four metals and solutions of different salts. She recorded some of her results in a table.

✓ shows that a reaction took place

✗ shows that no reaction took place

solutions \ metals	copper	iron	magnesium	zinc
copper sulphate	✗	✓	✓	
iron sulphate	✗	✗	✓	✓
magnesium sulphate	✗		✗	
zinc sulphate	✗	✗	✓	✗

(a) The four metals have different reactivities.

   (i) Use the information in the table to put the four metals in a reactivity series.

   most reactive metal ....

   ....

   ....

   least reactive metal ....   *1 mark*

   (ii) Use the reactivity series to complete the table by writing in ✓ or ✗ in the **three** empty boxes.   *2 marks*

(b)   Copper reacts with silver nitrate solution.

   (i)   Complete the word equation for the reaction:

      copper + silver nitrate $\longrightarrow$ .... + ... *2 marks*

   (ii)   Platinum does **not** react with silver nitrate.
         Put the metals platinum, copper and silver in the correct order according
         to their reactivity.

         most reactive ....

                       ....

         least reactive ....   *1 mark*

(c)   In many houses the hot water pipes are made from copper and the boiler is
      made from iron.
      Which of these metals will corrode first? Explain your answer.

      ....

      .... *1 mark*

                                                                    Maximum 7 marks

24   A group of pupils recorded
      some different characteristics
      of pupils in their class.

      The table below shows their results.

name	gender	height, in cm	mass, in kg	hand span, in cm	arm span, in cm	eye colour
Julie	girl	152	48	17.2	160	blue
Laura	girl	157	54	15.0	141	green
Aftab	boy	159	49	18.4	172	brown
Jenna	girl	144	46	17.4	161	hazel
Barry	boy	148	49	17.4	162	blue
Oliver	boy	172	57	21.5	204	brown
Safina	girl	155	48	16.8	158	brown
Maria	girl	154	50	17.9	166	green
Amanat	girl	162	46	16.2	150	brown
Thomas	boy	157	49	19.9	186	blue

(a)   Oliver concluded that boys do **not** have green eyes.
       Explain why his conclusion is **not** justified.

       -- *1 mark*

(b)   Name **two continuous** variables in their table.

       1 ---   2 --- *1 mark*

(c)   Look at the
       scatter graphs
       below.

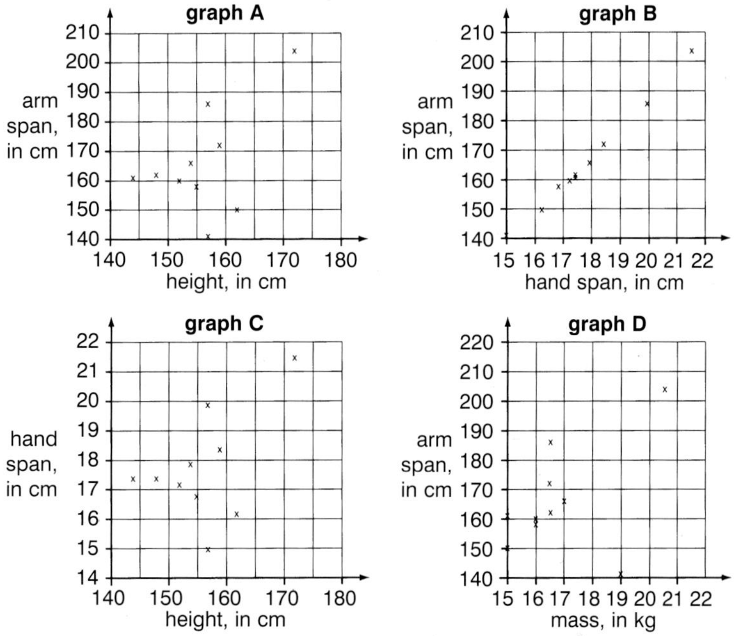

Use the data in the scatter graphs to show whether each of the conclusions
below is **true**, **false** or you **cannot tell**.

conclusions	true or false or cannot tell
Graph C shows that the shortest pupil has the smallest hand span.	---
Graph B shows the strongest correlation between two variables.	---
Graph A looks similar to graph C because of the high correlation of arm span to hand span.	---
Boys are generally taller than girls.	---

2 marks

Maximum 4 marks

THIS IS THE END OF THE TIER 5–7 PAPER

Paper 1

THIS IS THE START OF THE TIER 3–6 PAPER

Question 1

Part	Mark	Answer	Comments	What's this question looking for?
(a)	1	E	• Fish have gills, which enable them to extract oxygen from water.	*This question is testing your understanding of how variation (differences) between human beings can have both environmental and inherited causes.*
(b)	1	B or D or H	• Plants produce seeds.	
(c)	1	A or C or F or G	• Animals, which need oxygen for aerobic respiration, use their lungs for this purpose.	
(d)	2	E and F	• Fish and amphibians lay their eggs in water. • Answers may be in either order.	See page 6 in Unit 2, Revision Session 1 of *Collins Revision Guide KS3 Science*
(e)	2	E and G	• Fish and reptiles are covered in scales. • Answers may be in either order.	
Total	**7**			

Question 2

Part	Mark	Answer	Comments	What's this question looking for?
(a)	1	0	• The table shows that the first lettuce seed planted at 5°C germinated on day 5. This means that none had germinated by day 3.	*This question is testing your knowledge and understanding of some of the central aspects of Scientific Enquiry (Sc1); in particular the importance of planning, data collection and arriving at conclusions based on sufficient evidence.*
(b)	1	Any one from: • How many seeds germinated at different temperatures? • How many seeds grew or started to grow at different temperatures? • How long does it take seeds to grow **or** germinate at different temperatures?	• Temperature is the independent variable and you must identify this in the question which you think the children are investigating. • The dependent variable is either the number of seeds germinating or the time taken for the seeds to germinate. • Your answer must include both the dependent and the independent variable.	
(c)	2	true cannot tell false false	• Two lettuce seeds germinated on day 2. • You are not told the total number of seeds planted. • One lettuce seed germinated on day 5. • Two lettuce seeds germinated on day 2 at 25°C but the first seed at 15°C did not germinate until day 4. • You will get both marks if all four answers are correct. You will get one mark if two or three answers are correct. • Make sure that you do not tick more than one box in any of the four rows. If you do, you will not get credit for that row.	
Total	**4**			

60

Question 3

Part	Mark	Answer	Comments	What's this question looking for?
(a)	1	respiratory system	• An organ system is a group of organs which act together to fulfil a particular function. • Breathing is the way by which oxygen is obtained for aerobic respiration. • Make sure you only tick one box. If more than one box is ticked you will not get the mark.	*This question is testing your understanding of the role of lung structure in gas exchange.*
(b)	2	Part A : windpipe or trachea Part B : lung	• The trachea (windpipe) connects the nose and mouth with the lungs. • The lungs are two large organs inside the chest cavity, which are the sites of gas exchange.	
(c)	1	ribs	• The rib cage surrounds the chest cavity providing protection for the organs inside.	
(d) (i)	1	filtration	• The particles of sawdust are too large to pass through the material of the mask. • Air passes through the mask enabling the man to breathe, but it prevents the sawdust getting into his mouth.	
(d) (ii)	1	Any one from: • He might choke, cough, sneeze or get a sore throat; • It could cause cancer or lung disease; • He would have difficulty breathing; • His lungs might be damaged; • His airways could be blocked.	• The sawdust will build up in his mouth causing one of these responses to the irritation.	
Total	6			

Question 4

Part	Mark	Answer	Comments	What's this question looking for?
(a)	1 1	One line from 'Poisonous' to label S. One line from 'Corrosive' to label T.	• Hazard labels provide a visible warning of the possible dangers of using a particular chemical. • Make sure that you only draw one line from each description to one of the labels.	*This question is testing your ability to recognise that there are hazards in living things, materials and physical processes, and assess risks and take action to reduce risks to yourself and others.*
(b)	1	orange or red	• The additional information on the label confirms that this substance is an acid and is an irritant. • The chart shows the colour of universal indicator in a weakly acid solution is orange. • A bottle of kitchen cleaner is unlikely to be strongly acidic due to the health risk it might cause to the users.	
(b) (ii)	1	Q	• This kitchen cleaner is weakly acidic but is most hazardous because it is an irritant. • You will also get the mark if your answer is label T.	
Total	**4**			

Question 5

Part	Mark	Answer	Comments	What's this question looking for?
(a)	3		• Aluminium is used for bicycle frames because it is strong but lightweight. • Gold is used for jewellery because it does not react very easily. • Steel is used for compass needles because it is a magnetic material. • You will get one mark for each pair of lines correctly linking the metal to its use and then to its property.	*This question is testing your knowledge of how elements vary widely in their physical properties, including magnetic properties, and thermal and electrical conductivity, and how these properties can be used to classify elements as metals or non-metals.*
(b) (i)	1	Copper does not react with water.	• Whilst the other three statements are true this is the one which makes copper most suitable for this purpose. • Make sure you only tick one box. If more than one box is ticked you will not get the mark.	See page 17 in Unit 2, Revision Session 4 of *Collins Revision Guide KS3 Science*
(b) (ii)	1	Any one from: • It is a poor thermal conductor; • It is a good thermal insulator; • It prevents heat loss.	• Plastic foam is used to wrap hot water pipes because it prevents thermal energy being lost from the copper pipes.	
Total	**5**			

Question 6

Part	Mark	Answer	Comments	What's this question looking for?
(a)	1	40 g	• The ice has undergone a physical change from solid to liquid. During this sort of change mass is conserved.	*This question is testing your knowledge of when physical changes take place, mass is conserved and that the particle theory of matter can be used to explain the properties of solids, liquids and gases.*
(b) (i)	1	It had evaporated.	• Even in water at room temperature some molecules have sufficient energy to escape from the surface of the liquid and turn into water vapour. This process is called evaporation.	
(b) (ii)	2	Any one from: • It got warmer; • There was a breeze; • It got less humid or drier.	• The rate of evaporation from the beaker will change due to changes in the local conditions. • The water molecules evaporating from the beaker need sufficient energy to do so and also need space into which they can evaporate. • Lower humidity and faster moving air provide the space directly above the beaker for the water molecules to escape into.	See page 21 in Unit 2, Revision Session 5 of *Collins Revision Guide KS3 Science*
Total	4			

Question 7

Part	Mark	Answer	Comments	What's this question looking for?
(a) (i)	1	sedimentary	• Sedimentary rocks are formed when sediments, such as sand and mud, settle out and are compressed and cemented together by the weight of the sediment above.	*This question is testing your knowledge of how igneous, sedimentary and metamorphic rocks are formed and how the forces generated by the freezing of water can lead to the physical weathering of rocks.*
(a) (ii)	1	igneous	• Igneous rocks are formed when magma (molten rock from inside the Earth) cools and forms crystalline rocks. They are very hard and have a speckled appearance.	
(b)	1 1	The temperature falls below freezing point. Expansion forces the cracks in the rock to open.	• The temperature must fall below 0^0C for the water in the crack to freeze. • Water is the only substance which expands when it freezes. This expansion exerts forces on the sides of the crack causing it become larger. • Make sure that you only tick two boxes. If you tick more you will lose a mark for every additional box ticked.	See page 58 in Unit 3, Revision Session 5 of *Collins Revision Guide KS3 Science*
Total	4			

Question 8

Part	Mark	Answer	Comments	What's this question looking for?
(a)	1	ruler	• The ruler is the only piece of equipment which you can use to measure the length of an object. • Only tick one box. If you tick more boxes you will not be awarded the mark.	*This question is testing your knowledge and understanding of some of the central aspects of Scientific Enquiry (Sc1); in particular the importance of planning, in investigative work and how to use data to draw conclusions.*
(b)	1	Any one from: • The tubes had different widths; • The tubes had different bores; • The tubes had different shapes/sizes; • He blew in different ways; • They were made from different thicknesses of paper; • They were made from different paper;	• A fair test is one where the results are due to changing only one factor. • If several things about the tubes are different then it will not be possible to identify which factor causes the changes in the pitch of the sounds produced.	
(c)	1	The longer tube will make a lower sound.	• The other three are statements of what is known at the present. The word 'prediction' suggests what will happen in the future. • Only tick one box. If you tick more boxes you will not be awarded the mark.	
(d)	1	5	• Read the result directly from the table. The high pitched sound is produced by the tube which is 5 cm long.	
Total	**4**			

Question 9

Part	Mark	Answer	Comments	What's this question looking for?
(a)	1	Any one from: • light travels faster than sound; • sound travels more slowly than light; • light travels faster; • sound travels slower.	• Sound travels through air at about 330 m/s and light travels at about 300 million m/s. • The light from the flash of lightning would reach you long before the sound it makes.	*This question is testing your knowledge and understanding of some of the central aspects of Scientific Enquiry (Sc1); in particular the importance of methods of obtaining, presenting and considering evidence.*
(b)(i)	1	A bar on the bar chart standing over the letter D with its top halfway between the 8 and 10 seconds lines.	• The table states that there are 9 seconds between seeing the flash of lightning D, and hearing the thunder. • The bar on the bar chart indicates this time by being drawn up to the middle of the gap between the 8 and 10 second lines.	

Part	Mark	Answer	Comments	What's this question looking for?
(b)(ii)	1	Flash of lightning C.	• The flash of lightning closest to Omar will be the one from which the sound takes the shortest time to reach him after seeing the flash.	
(b)(iii)	1	Any one from: • the storm became closer then moved further away; • towards then away from Omar; • the distance decreased then increased; • the storm passed over/by.	• The pattern in the table shows that, with each successive lightning flash, the time between seeing the light and hearing the sound decreases from 8 to 5 to 3 seconds and then increases to 9 and 13 and 16.5 seconds. • This shows that the storm got closer to Omar and then moved further away.	
Total	4			

Question 10

Part	Mark	Answer	Comments	What's this question looking for?
(a)	1	Gravity or weight.	• All objects have a weight due to the gravitational force of the Earth which attracts them towards the centre of the Earth.	*This question is testing your understanding that the weight of an object on Earth is the result of the gravitational attraction between its mass and that of the Earth.*
(b)(i)	1	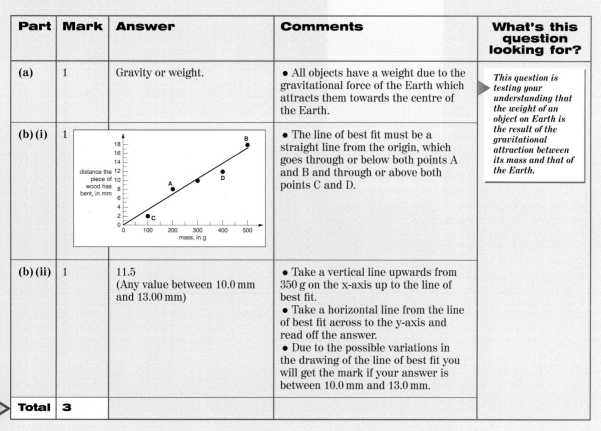	• The line of best fit must be a straight line from the origin, which goes through or below both points A and B and through or above both points C and D.	
(b)(ii)	1	11.5 (Any value between 10.0 mm and 13.00 mm)	• Take a vertical line upwards from 350 g on the x-axis up to the line of best fit. • Take a horizontal line from the line of best fit across to the y-axis and read off the answer. • Due to the possible variations in the drawing of the line of best fit you will get the mark if your answer is between 10.0 mm and 13.0 mm.	
Total	3			

THIS IS THE START OF THE TIER 5–7 PAPER

Question 11

Part	Mark	Answer	Comments	What's this question looking for?
(a)	1	Minerals or mineral salts.	• You are asked to name the type of substance that the oak tree takes from the soil. • 'Phosphate', 'nitrate' or just 'salts' will also get the mark. • Naming specific elements like nitrogen or potassium will not get the mark nor will a general reference to 'food'.	*This question is testing your knowledge and understanding of plant nutrition and growth and how some organisms are adapted to survive in their habitat.*
(b)	1	Any one from: • It covers a wide area; • They can reach a long way from the plant; • They can reach deeper; • They have a large surface area; • They have more root hairs.	• The larger the size of the root system the better able the tree is to absorb water from the soil.	
(c)	1	Any one from: • Photosynthesis cannot take place; • Photosynthesis takes place in the leaves; • No food is being made.	• The leaves of the tree are the main sites of photosynthesis – the process that produces biomass from carbon dioxide and water. • Having lost all of its leaves the tree is unable to produce biomass for growth.	
(d)	2	Any two from: • It is camouflaged; • It is shaped like a twig; • It is the same colour/pattern as the twig; • The birds cannot see it; • It does not get eaten.	• The caterpillar has adapted to surviving in this habitat by making itself look like a twig of an oak tree. • It is much harder for predators to identify the caterpillar because it 'blends in' to surroundings and therefore is less likely to get eaten.	
Total	5			

Question 12

Part	Mark	Answer	Comments	What's this question looking for?
(a)	1	Q (1941–1947)	• If large amounts of alcohol, drunk daily, causes cirrhosis of the liver one of the reasons fewer people suffer with this disease is because alcohol is difficult to obtain. • It is likely that a fall in the number of people suffering with this disease will be at times when there is least alcohol to drink. • The dip in the graph shows when this was.	*This question is testing your knowledge of how the abuse of alcohol, solvents and other drugs affects health.*

Part	Mark	Answer	Comments	What's this question looking for?
(b)	1	It affects the nervous system.	• The most important feature of any drug either prescribed, legally available or illegal, is that it affects the nervous system. • Make sure you only tick one box. If more than one box is ticked you will not get the mark.	
(c)(i)	1	The chances of having an accident increase. The rate of increase gets faster the more alcohol is in the blood.	• The graph shows that as the amount of alcohol in the blood increases the the chances of having an accident become greater. • The gradient of the graph increases rapidly for small increases in the amount of alcohol in the blood. So for small increases in the amount of alcohol in the blood there are increasingly large increases in the chances of an accident.	
(c)(ii)	1	Alcohol increases the time a person takes to react.	• Alcohol causes people to be less aware of and less concerned about their actions. They are therefore slow to react to potential dangers. • Make sure you only tick one box. If more than one box is ticked you will not get the mark.	
Total	5			

Question 13

Part	Mark	Answer	Comments	What's this question looking for?
(a)	1	Red blood cell.	• This disc-shaped cell has a large surface area, due to the concave surface, for carrying substances around the blood system.	*This question is testing your knowledge and understanding of the ways in which some cells, including ciliated epithelial cells, sperm, ova and root hair cells, are adapted to their functions.*
(b)(i)	1	B	• This is a typical plant cell containing chloroplasts, the containers of the green substance chlorophyll, which is needed for photosynthesis to take place.	
(b)(ii)	1	A	• This is a ciliated epithelial cell. These cells line the windpipe and lungs. The small hairs move mucus, which traps bacteria and dust, along the windpipe.	See page 83 in Unit 4, Revision Session 2 of *Collins Revision Guide KS3 Science*
(c)(i)	1	Testis or testicle	• Cell E is a sperm cell. These are produced in the testes in males.	
(c)(ii)	1	Leaf or stem or any green part of a plant.	• Cell B is a typical plant cell containing chloroplasts, which give the green parts of all plants their colour.	
Total	5			

Question 14

Part	Mark	Answer	Comments	What's this question looking for?
(a) (i)	1	Any one from: • They increase; • They expand; • They get bigger.	• As objects get hotter the particles within them move faster and further apart making the object larger. This process is called expansion.	*This question is testing your knowledge of how the particle theory of matter can be used to explain the properties of solids, liquids and gases.*
(a) (ii)	1	They get smaller or they will decrease or they shrink.	• As the concrete sections get larger due to expansion the gaps between then get smaller as the sections get closer together.	See page 58 in Unit 3, Revision Session 5 of *Collins Revision Guide KS3 Science*
(a) (iii)	1	They might bend or crack or break up.	• Without gaps between them the concrete sections would expand against each other and the forces produced could cause damage to the road sections.	
(b)	1	So that it can be pushed out as the gaps get smaller due to the concrete expanding.	• The gaps between the concrete sections must be filled with a substance that is flexible enough to respond to the changing size of the gap as the road sections expand. • The tar softens when it gets warm and can be pushed out of the gap as the road sections get closer together.	
Total	4			

Question 15

Part	Mark	Answer	Comments	What's this question looking for?
(a)	1 1	Purple Any one from: • It changes colour in both acids and alkalis; • It goes pink in acid (pH1) and blue in alkali (pH10).	• The purple flower is the only one which responds differently to the three different solutions. • There is one mark for the correct colour and a second for the correct explanation.	*This question is testing your knowledge of how to use indicators to classify solutions as acidic, neutral and alkaline and how to separate mixtures into their constituents using chromatography.*
(b) (i)	1	Chromatography	• As the liquid spreads out across the filter paper different solids will be unable to remain in solution and will become visible as a ring on the paper.	See page 24 in Unit 2, Revision Session 6 of *Collins Revision Guide KS3 Science*
(c)	3	dissolved solvent red	• The coloured substances dissolved in the liquid • A liquid which dissolves a solid is called a solvent. • Two different coloured substances formed the two rings on the filter paper testing the solution from the red petals. • The three answers must be in the correct order.	
Total	6			

Question 16

Part	Mark	Answer	Comments	What's this question looking for?
(a)	1	A letter E marked on the diagram showing that the Earth has travelled through 90° of its orbit. 	• One Earth year is 12 months. Three months is one quarter of a year so the Earth will have travelled one quarter of a rotation (90°) around the Sun in three months. • Make sure that you mark the position of the Earth, E, on the path of the orbit on the diagram.	*This question is testing your understanding of the movements of planets around the Sun and how these relate to gravitational forces.* See page 70 in Unit 3, Revision Session 9 of *Collins Revision Guide KS3 Science*
(b) (i)	1	A letter M marked on the diagram showing that Mars has travelled through less than 90° of its orbit.	• Mars takes 1.9 Earth years to make one orbit of the Sun. So in three months Mars will have travelled only about 45° around its orbit. You will get this mark by showing that it is less than the distance travelled by the Earth. • Make sure that you mark the position of Mars, M, on the path of the orbit on the diagram.	
(b) (ii)	1	Any one from: • Outer planets move more slowly; • Outer planets take longer to orbit; • Mars has a longer year; • The orbit of Mars is longer; • The outer planets have further to go.	• The orbital distance of planets further from the Sun is greater than those close to the Sun.	
(c) (i)	1	A letter V marked on the diagram to show that Venus has travelled through more than 90° and less than 180° of its orbit.	• Venus takes 0.6 Earth years to make one orbit of the Sun. So in three months Venus will have travelled about 150° around its orbit. You will get this mark by showing that it is more than the distance travelled by the Earth. • Make sure that you mark the position of Venus, V, on the path of the orbit on the diagram.	
(c) (ii)	1	Any one from: • Inner planets move more quickly; • It moves more quickly; • Inner planets take less time to orbit; • Venus has a shorter year; • The orbit of Venus is shorter; • The inner planets have less far to go.	• The orbital distance of planets closer to the Sun is less than those further away from the Sun.	
Total	5			

Question 17

Part	Mark	Answer	Comments	What's this question looking for?
(a)	1	friction	• Friction is the force produced when two substances that are touching move past each other.	*This question is testing your knowledge of:*
(b)(i)	1	Any one from: • Energy stored in the rubber band gets less; • The tension in the rubber band decreased; • The force exerted by the rubber band gets less.	• The elastic band stored the energy, which was used to wind it up. As the elastic band unwinds this energy is used to drive the cotton reel along the tabletop. • The slowing down is a result of the difference between the energy released and the resistance due to friction getting less and less as the cottonreel moves along.	• *the ways in which frictional forces affect motion;* • *the ways in which energy can be usefully transferred and stored;* • *the fact that energy dissipation reduces its availability as a resource.*
(b)(ii)	1	Any one from: • Give the band more turns; • Twist the rubber band more; • Wind up the rubber band more.	• By storing more energy in the elastic band it is possible to make this vehicle move faster.	
Total	**3**			

Question 18

Part	Mark	Answer	Comments	What's this question looking for?
(a)	1	A and B	• These were the two models where the length of the string was the same but the mass of plasticine in the swing was different.	*This question is testing your knowledge and understanding of some of the central aspects of Scientific Enquiry (Sc1); in particular the importance of and considering and evaluating evidence.*
(b)(i)	1	Any one from: • The longer the string, the longer it takes; • The longer the string the more time it takes.	• From the results for A, C and D in the table you can see that as the string is made longer the time for 10 complete swings gets longer. • You have to make reference to both length and time to get this mark.	
(b)(ii)	1	A and C and D	• These three all have the same mass of plasticine and are all different lengths. • Your answers can be in any order but all three must be correct to get the mark.	
(c)	1	E = 10.0 F = from 18 to 25 • Both correct answers are needed for this mark.	• If the mass in the swing has no effect on the time then with a length of 25 cm the time for 10 complete swings will be the same as for A and B. • As the time taken for 10 complete swings increases as the string gets longer, the increase in length from 75 to 100 might increase the time taken as much as increasing the length from 50 to 75. • It will be longer than the time taken by D and the pattern in the table shows that it is likely to be in the order of 20 seconds.	
Total	**4**			

THIS IS THE END OF THE TIER 3–6 PAPER

Question 19

Part	Mark	Answer	Comments	What's this question looking for?
(a) (i)	1	refraction	• The process by which light changes direction as it passes from one medium to another is called refraction.	*This question is testing your knowledge of:*
(a) (ii)	1	dispersion	• The seven colours of the visible spectrum appear on the screen because each of them has been refracted by different amounts as they pass through the glass block. The name for this process is dispersion.	• *How light is refracted at the boundary between two different materials;*
(b)	1	Only the green part would be seen.	• The green chlorophyll solution absorbs all colours of light except green, which passes through the liquid.	• *The effect of coloured filters on white light;*
	1	Other colours are absorbed or removed by the green solution.	• You will get one mark for describing what would be seen on the screen and the second mark for the explanation.	• *The function of chloroplasts in plant cells;* • *How some organisms are adapted to survive daily and seasonal changes in their habitats.*
(c)	1	Any one from: • To break down the cell walls; • To break open the cells; • Because the green substance is inside the cells or chloroplasts; • To break up the chloroplasts.	• The chlorophyll is contained within chloroplasts of the buttercup leaves. Grinding the leaves releases the chlorophyll from the leaves which is dissolved by the solvent.	See: page 64 in Unit 3, Revision Session 7; page 48 in Unit 3, Revision Session 2 of *Collins Revision Guide KS3 Science*
(d)	1	Any one from: • Dog's Mercury has a higher rate of photosynthesis than buttercups in low light; • Buttercups have a lower rate of photosynthesis than Dog's Mercury in low light; • Buttercups reach their maximum rate of photosynthesis at higher light intensities; • Dog's Mercury reaches its maximum rate of photosynthesis at lower light intensities;	• As Dog's Mercury grows in woodland it is exposed to much lower light intensities because of the shade produced by the surrounding trees. In this habitat buttercups will not grow very well because they will not be able to receive the intensity of light which they need to reach their maximum rate of photosynthesis. • A statement about one or other of the plants will not be enough. You must make a comparison between the rate of photosynthesis in Dog's Mercury and in buttercups to get this mark.	
Total	6			

Question 20

Part	Mark	Answer	Comments	What's this question looking for?
(a) (i)	1	tissue	• A group of similar cells which work together is called a tissue. There are many different types of tissue in the body. Skin, nerves and tendons are three examples.	*This question is testing your knowledge of the ways in which some cells are adapted to their function and the effects of smoking on health.*
(a) (ii)	1	Mucus traps bacteria or dust.	• Mucus is a sticky substance which covers the lining of the windpipe. Any bacteria or dust landing on it will stick to its surface.	See page 83 in Unit 4, Revision Session 2 of *Collins Revision Guide KS3 Science*
	1	Cilia move mucus out of the lungs or windpipe.	• The cilia move gently in waves and carry the mucus along and out of the lungs and windpipe.	
(b)	2	Any two from: • Mucus will build up; • Airways will be partially blocked; • Coughing; • Lungs can become infected; • Bacteria are not removed.	• The cigarette smoke will cause a variety of problems arising from too much mucus being in the airway and the cilia not being able to remove it because they are damaged.	
(c)	2	Any two from: **Nicotine** • Causes addiction; • Causes raised blood pressure; • Causes raised heart rate; • Causes cilia to stop working. **Tar** • Causes cancer; • Blocks the airways; • Clogs the cilia; • Builds up in the alveoli. **Carbon particles** • Cause coughing; • Cause cancer. **Carbon monoxide** • Causes reduced amounts of oxygen carried in the blood.	• The four harmful substances in cigarette smoke are nicotine, tar, carbon particles and carbon monoxide. • You will have to give both the name of the substance and its effect for each of these two marks.	
Total	**7**			

Question 21

Part	Mark	Answer	Comments	What's this question looking for?
(a) (i)	1	C	• A substance made up of two or more different elements, which are chemically combined, is called a compound. • The molecules made up of two different elements show that this substance is a compound.	

Part	Mark	Answer	Comments	What's this question looking for?
(a) (ii)	1	D	• A substance made up of two or more different elements, which are not chemically combined, is called a mixture. • The black coloured atoms are of a different element but are contained within the structure of the other atoms rather than chemically combined.	*This question is testing your understanding of the particle theory and how it can be used to explain the properties of solids, liquids and gases and how elements combine to form compounds as well as existing in mixtures where the constituents are not chemically combined.*
(a) (iii)	1	A and B	• Elements are made up entirely of one type of atom. • Even though the atoms are joined into molecules in substance B they are all atoms of the same type. • Some elements, mostly gases such as oxygen, exist as molecules. • The two answers may be in either order but both are required for the mark.	See: page 58 in Unit 3, Revision Session 5; page 55 in Unit 3, Revision Session 4 of *Collins Revision Guide KS3 Science*
(a) (iv)	1	A and D	• Gases such as B and C are unlikely to be good thermal conductors because of the large distances between the particles. • The atoms in these two substances are packed closely together so, depending on the nature of the types of atoms, they could be good thermal conductors. • The two answers may be in either order but both are required for the mark.	
(a) (v)	1	C	• Carbon dioxide is a gas at room temperature. • Its name tells you two things. Firstly, that it is made up of two different elements, carbon and oxygen, but also that there are two oxygen atoms to every carbon atom. That is why it is carbon **di**oxide rather than carbon oxide. • This is the only substance which is a molecule made up of three atoms, two of which are the same.	
(b) (i)	1	The same	• As there was no reaction between the two substances the number of molecules in the mixture must be the same as the total number in substances B and C.	
(b) (ii)	1	A random mixed arrangement of both types of molecule should be drawn with the molecules not touching each other.	• The two substances will move freely past and around each other to fill all the space available to them.	
Total	7			

Question 22

Part	Mark	Answer	Comments	What's this question looking for?
(a)	1	aluminium oxide	• The aluminium displaces the iron from the iron oxide because aluminium is more reactive than iron.	*This question is testing your knowledge of how to summarise reactions by word equations, about the displacement reactions and how a reactivity series of metals can be determined by considering these reactions.*
(b)	1	aluminium iron copper	• Aluminium is more reactive than iron. • Copper does not displace iron from iron oxide so it is less reactive than iron. • The three metals must be in the correct order to get the mark.	
(c)(i)	1	no reaction or nothing	• From the reactivity series you can see that zinc is less reactive than calcium. It will not displace calcium from the calcium oxide so no reaction will take place.	See page 97 in Unit 4, Revision Session 6 of *Collins Revision Guide KS3 Science*
(c)(ii)	1	Any one from: • Zinc (Zn) • Silver (Ag) • Magnesium (Mg)	• Any metal lower than magnesium in the reactivity series will not react with a solution of magnesium sulphate. • Magnesium itself will not react with the solution of magnesium sulphate.	
(d)	1 1	zinc + oxygen → zinc oxide	• The left-hand side of the word equation identifies the reactants. • When substances burn in air they are being oxidised – the oxide of the metal is formed. • The right-hand side of the word equation identifies the products.	
Total	**6**			

Question 23

Part	Mark	Answer	Comments	What's this question looking for?
(a)(i)	1	1.44	• Speed = distance/time • Speed = 260/180 • Speed = 1.44 m/min	*This question is testing your understanding of how to determine the speed of a moving object and if you can use the quantitative relationship between speed, distance and time.*
(a)(ii)	1	0.024	• If the speed of the tape is 1.44 m/min it will have travelled 1.44 m in 60 seconds. • Speed = 1.44/60 m/s • Speed = 0.024 m/s	
(b)(i)	1	240.7 s or 241 s or 4 minutes	• Time = distance/speed • Time = 260/1.08 • Time = 240.7 s	
(b)(ii)	1	Any one from: • It takes time to reach the maximum speed; • It slows down before the end; • It is not the average speed.	• The question tells you that the different motor has a <u>maximum</u> speed of 1.08 m/s. This means that at some other times it is operating more slowly than this. • As a result the time taken to rewind the tape must be longer than 240.7 seconds.	
Total	4			

Question 24

Part	Mark	Answer	Comments	What's this question looking for?
(a)(i)	1	25	• Pressure = force/area. • Pressure = 175 N/7 cm^2 = 25 N/cm^2. • You will also get the mark if you leave your answer as 175/7.	*This question is testing your understanding of the quantitative relationship between force, area and pressure and your ability to apply it to real life situations.*
(b)	1	Any one from: • greater than 27 N/cm^2; • greater than the pressure in the tyre.	• If air is to move into the tyre from the pump the pressure in the pump must be greater than the pressure in the tyre.	See page 102 in Unit 4, Revision Session 8 of *Collins Revision Guide KS3 Science*
(c)	1	2850	• Pressure = force/area • Force = pressure x area. • Force = 30 N/cm^2 x 95 cm^2. • Force = 2850 N	
Total	3			

THIS IS THE END OF THE TIER 5–7 PAPER

Paper 2

Question 1

Part	Mark	Answer	Comments	What's this question looking for?
(a)(i)	1	B	• Light travels in straight lines. Both lines A and C are curved.	*This question is testing if you know that light travels in a straight line at a finite speed in a uniform medium and that you understand the relationship between the loudness of a sound and the amplitude of the vibration causing it.*
(a)(ii)	1	About one hundred millionth of a second	• The speed of light is 300000000 m/s. So to travel the short distance from the spotlight to the actor will not take very long. • Only tick one box. If you tick more boxes you will not be awarded the mark.	
(b)(i)	1	The actor's voice is quieter for those people in the back row.	• Energy from the sound of the actor's voice is lost as it moves through the air. His voice is quieter because less energy reaches the people sitting in the back row. • Any answer indicating that his voice is softer or fainter or that the people in the back row have difficulty hearing him will get the mark.	
(b)(ii)	1	The time taken for his voice to reach the audience is **longer**.	• The actor is further away from the audience so the sound from his voice has further to travel and it will take slightly longer than when he is at the front of the stage.	
Total	**4**			

Question 2

Part	Mark	Answer	Comments	What's this question looking for?
(a)(i)	1	An arrow pointing towards the right.	• The cat is moving from left to right through the door. It must push the cat-flap away from the door as it passes through the gap.	*This question is testing if you know that forces cause objects to turn about a pivot and your understanding of magnetic fields as regions of space where magnetic materials experience forces, including the fact that like magnetic poles repel and unlike poles attract.*
(a)(ii)	1	Label line, identified with the letter, P, touching or leading towards the ball and socket hinge.	• The pivot is the point about which the cat-flap rotates in order for it to open and allow the cat through the door. • You would also get the mark by writing the letter P alongside the pivot point on the diagram, without the label line, provided the letter is within 1 cm of it.	

Part	Mark	Answer	Comments	What's this question looking for?
(b)	1	N S	• You must label both N and S poles of the magnet to get the mark.	
(c)	1	Any one from: • grease; • oil; • lubricant.	• Squeaks caused by friction can be prevented by applying a lubricant, such as grease or oil to the pivot.	
Total	**4**			

Question 3

Part	Mark	Answer	Comments	What's this question looking for?
(a)	1	2 hours	• Use the plotted line on the graph. Read up from 96dB on the horizontal scale to the plotted line and across to the left to find the answer.	*This question is testing your ability to use diagrams, tables, charts and graphs, including lines of best fit, to identify and describe patterns or relationships in data. It is also testing your knowledge of the effects of loud sounds on the ear.*
(b)	1	It would damage or burst the eardrum.	• Very loud sounds cause the eardrum to vibrate violently which could cause it to be stretched or broken. • You will also get the mark if you refer to any particular part of the middle and inner ear being damaged or this causing deafness, tinnitus or ringing in the ear.	
(c)(i)	1	92dB	• Read across from 5 hours on the vertical scale and down from the point where this line meets the plotted graph to get the answer.	
(c)(ii)	1	Any one from: • they make the sound quieter; • they absorb the sound; • they prevent damage to the eardrum.	• Ear plugs provide a physical barrier between the sounds and the eardrum. They reduce the energy entering the ears and prevent them from being damaged.	
Total	**4**			

Question 4

Part	Mark	Answer	Comments	What's this question looking for?
(a)	1	'Glossy' would have more bubbles than the others.	• If you were correct, the claim on the poster would have to be demonstrated. • To get the mark you would have to be specific and say that this washing-up liquid did make 'more' bubbles than the others not just many or lots of bubbles.	*This question is testing your knowledge and understanding of some of the central aspects of Scientific Enquiry (Sc1); in particular the importance of ideas and evidence in science along with the importance of planning in investigative work.*
(b)	1	Any one from: • to make the test fair; • if they use different amounts it will be unfair; • it is a controlled experiment.	• In order to be able to arrive at a valid conclusion you must undertake a fair test. • You will have controlled the volume of washing-up liquid used in the test-tube so that you will be able to compare the outcomes of your experiment.	
(c)	1	Any one from: • they could not compare the amounts of bubbles; • they could not tell which was better; • they could not tell the difference; • they could not know which made the most bubbles.	• There was so much washing-up liquid in each test-tube that the results did not allow you to tell the difference between the effects of each one. • In order to get results which allow comparison you would have had to reduce the amount of washing-up liquid used in each test-tube.	
(d)	1	Any one from: • Shine will have the most bubbles; • Shine will make the most froth; • Shine would produce more bubbles than Glossy.	• The test-tube containing 'Shine' has the most bubbles. If this result supports Jane's prediction then she must have predicted that this was going to be the case.	
Total	**4**			

Question 5

Part	Mark	Answer	Comments	What's this question looking for?
(a)	1 1 1	(table)	• The cabbage water was purple when water was added to it. This colour demonstrates that the test liquid was neutral. • If the test liquid added to the cabbage water was acidic it would turn the cabbage water red. • The cabbage water was blue when washing-up liquid was added to it. This colour shows that the test liquid was alkaline.	*This question is testing your ability to use tables to identify relationships in data and to use indicators to classify solutions as acidic, neutral and alkaline.*
(b)	1	indicators	• This is the name given to any chemical which changes colour in acids and alkalis. • Only tick one box. If you tick more boxes you will not be awarded the mark.	
Total	**4**			

Table within Question 5 (a):

liquid added to the cabbage water	colour of the cabbage water	is the liquid acidic, alkaline or neutral?
water	purple	**neutral**
lemon juice	**red**	acidic
washing-up liquid	blue	**alkaline**

Question 6

Part	Mark	Answer	Comments	What's this question looking for?
(a)(i)	1	magma	• This is the name for underground molten rock. • Make sure that you only use one of the three words provided as your answer.	*This question is testing your knowledge of:* • *the processes of formation of different types of rocks;* • *how the properties of elements can be used to classify them as metals or non-metals.*
(a)(ii)	1	igneous	• This is the name given to the rocks produced by volcanoes. • Make sure that you only use one of the three words provided as your answer.	
(b)(i)	1	Any one from: • thermal energy • electricity	• Being a non-metallic element, sulphur is not able to conduct either thermal energy or electricity in the way that metallic elements can.	See page 58 in Unit 3, Revision Session 5 of *Collins Revision Guide KS3 Science*
(b)(ii)	1 1	solid liquid	• You are told in the question that sulphur melts at 115^0C. • Melting is the process during which a substance changes from solid to liquid.	
(c)	1	oxygen	• Any substance that burns in air is reacting with the oxygen, which it contains.	
Total	**6**			

Question 7

Part	Mark	Answer	Comments	What's this question looking for?
(a)	1 1 1	solution insoluble solvent	• A solid dissolved in a liquid is called a solution. • An insoluble substance is one that will not dissolve in the liquid. • The liquid part of a solution is called the solvent. • Your answers must be in the correct order.	*This question is testing your knowledge of the differences in solubility of solutes in different solvents and how to separate mixtures into their constituent parts.*
(b)	1	Any one from: • filter it; • filtration; • pour off the liquid.	• Separating the white solid from the brown liquid is relatively easy because it has not dissolved in the liquid. • The brown liquid could be poured off leaving the white solid behind. • Emptying everything in the container into a funnel containing filter paper will allow the brown liquid to pass through but capture the white solid in the filter paper.	See page 24 in Unit 2, Revision Session 6 of *Collins Revision Guide KS3 Science*
(c)	1	It had evaporated.	• Water evaporates even at room temperature. As it does so, the brown substance dries out leaving the brown solid behind in the dish.	
(d)	1	condensing	• A vapour is the gaseous form of a substance, which exists below the boiling point of the liquid. • Condensation is the process by which a gas turns into a liquid.	
Total	**6**			

Question 8

Part	Mark	Answer	Comments	What's this question looking for?
(a) (i)	1	beaker C	• The waterweed in beaker C was in bright light. It would be able to use this light in the process of photosynthesis to grow well.	*This question is testing your understanding of what plants need for photosynthesis in order to produce biomass and oxygen and that nitrogen and other elements are required for plant growth.*
(a) (ii)	1	Any one from: • no light; • it was in the dark.	• You will not get the mark if you simply state that the plant was in the box. • The result of being in the box is that the plant is not exposed to light and that photosynthesis does not take place which causes the leaves to change from dark green to pale yellow.	See page 52 in Unit 3, Revision Session 3 of *Collins Revision Guide KS3 Science*
(b)	1	Any one from: • less light reached the lower plants; • plants need light to grow; • the water lilies blocked the light.	• Sunlight is not able to penetrate the water surface because it is covered by the large water lily leaves.	
(c) (i)	1	Any one from: • the waterweed in E will grow bigger than in D; • the waterweed in E will have more leaves than in D.	• Fertilizers contain the minerals plants need for healthy growth. • The waterweed in beaker E will have these minerals available and should grow more strongly than the waterweed in beaker D.	
(c) (ii)	1	minerals	• Plants need minerals such as nitrogen, potassium and phosphorus for healthy growth. • Only tick one box. If you tick more boxes you will not be awarded the mark.	
Total	**5**			

Question 9

Part	Mark	Answer	Comments	What's this question looking for?
(a)	1	A: insects	• The fly has a body in three sections, six legs and a pair of wings – a typical insect.	*This question is testing your ability to classify living things into the major taxonomic groups.*
	1	B: amphibians	• A frog has a smooth, damp skin, and lives both on land and in water – a typical amphibian.	See page 6 in Unit 2, Revision Session 1 of *Collins Revision Guide KS3 Science*
	1	C: molluscs	• A snail is a soft-bodied invertebrate with an unsegmented body – a typical mollusc.	
	1	D: reptiles	• A snake has hard dry scales and lays soft-shelled eggs on land – a typical reptile. • Only use the names from the list provided.	
(b) (i)	1 1	A C	• Invertebrates are animals without a backbone. • Your answers may be in either order.	
Total	**6**			

80

Question 10

Part	Mark	Answer	Comments	What's this question looking for?
(a)	1	The bowling ball, because it has the greatest mass or it is the heaviest.	• You must give the correct ball and the correct reason to be awarded the one mark. • Your answer must refer to the mass of the bowling ball. A general comment that it is bigger will not be enough to get this mark.	*This question is testing your knowledge and understanding of some of the central aspects of Scientific Enquiry (Sc1); in particular the importance of ideas and evidence in science. It is also testing your understanding that the weight of an object on Earth is the result of the gravitational attraction between its mass and that of the Earth.*
(b)	1	Any one from: • they are the same diameter; • they are the same size; • they produce the same air resistance or friction.	• In the first test, the balls vary in two ways – their mass and their size. • This test is fairer because it is possible to work out if mass makes a difference because the balls are the same size.	
(c) (i)	1	They would both reach the ground at the same time.	• This would be the result if Galileo were correct and the only factor affecting the falling objects is gravity.	
(c) (ii)	1	air resistance	• You would also get the mark if you called this force friction.	
(c) (iii)	2	Either: the feather and the hammer landed at the same time; there is no atmosphere or air resistance on the moon. Or: they would take longer to fall on the moon; because there is lower gravity than on the Earth.	• The moon does not have an atmosphere so the two objects will fall to the surface without being affected by air resistance. • The moon does have a gravitational attraction to all objects but it is much less than on the Earth. The two objects will fall to the surface but more slowly because they are being affected by a much smaller gravitational attraction.	
Total	**6**			

Question 11

Part	Mark	Answer	Comments	What's this question looking for?
(a)	1	pick-up wire metal wheel	• The diagram shows the circuit needed for the dodgem cars to work. • Both of these answers, in the correct order, are required for the mark.	*This question is testing your knowledge of how to design and construct series and parallel circuits.*

Part	Mark	Answer	Comments	What's this question looking for?
(b)	2	One mark is for drawing the two motors connected in parallel. One mark is for drawing one switch in series with each motor.	• The question tells you that the dodgem cars are connected in parallel. The part of the circuit for each car should be adjacent to each other and each part must contain a motor and a switch. • In both parts of the circuit the switches can be on either side of the motor but they must be in series with each other.	
(c)	1	Any one from: • it completes the circuit; • it acts as a switch; • it connects the motor to the power supply.	• The pedal controls the movement of the dodgem car because pressing it down completes the circuit, current flows and the motor moves the car forward.	
(d)	1	Any one from: • he does not complete the circuit; • he does not connect the floor to the wire mesh ceiling.	• The man looking after the dodgem cars is safe from electric shocks unless he connects himself to both sides of the circuit. He can walk on the metal floor in safety because he is only in contact with one side of the circuit.	
(e)(i)	1	It stops	• With a broken pick-up wire the dodgem car loses its connection to the circuit and no electricity is available to power the motor. It is not able to move.	
(e)(ii)	1	Any one from: • it continues to move; • it is not affected; • it does not stop.	• The circuit to this car remains intact and the car is able to continue moving.	
Total	7			

Question 12

Part	Mark	Answer	Comments	What's this question looking for?
(a)(i)	1 1	One mark for each correct row.	• Low pH values indicate acidic solutions, which turn universal indicator red. • High pH values indicate alkaline solutions, which turn universal indicator blue/purple.	*This question is testing your knowledge of how indicators are used to classify solutions as acidic, neutral or alkaline; how the pH scale is used to measure the acidity of a solution and one everyday application of neutralisation.*
(b)(i)	1	Any one from: • bicarbonate toothpaste; • washing soda.	• Bee stings are acidic so an alkaline substance is needed to neutralise their effects. The alkaline substances are those in the table with pH values greater than 7.	

Part	Mark	Answer	Comments	What's this question looking for?
(b) (ii)	1	Any one from: • vinegar; • lemon juice.	• Wasp stings are alkaline so an acidic substance is needed to neutralise their effects. The acidic substances are those in the table with pH values less than 7.	
Total	**4**			

Question 13

Part	Mark	Answer	Comments	What's this question looking for?
(a)	1	No **and** Any one from: • sulphuric acid did not cure scurvy; • not all of the sailors recovered; • only two pairs recovered; • only those with fruit related additions recovered; • some with the acid failed to recover; • a week is not long enough to show the effect.	• You need **both** the answer and the explanation to get the mark. • If both boxes are ticked then you will not get the mark even if your explanation is correct. • Any piece of evidence available from the table, which is not consistent with (is opposite to) the prediction made by James Lind will support the answer.	*This question is testing your knowledge and understanding of some of the central aspects of Scientific Enquiry (Sc1); in particular the importance of ideas and evidence in science along with the importance of planning in investigative work.*
(b) (i)	1	Any one from: • addition to their diet; • food **or** drink supplements; • type of acid.	• An independent variable is one which which is changed during the experiment. • You will not get the mark if you make vague reference to type of food or drink.	
(b) (ii)	1	Any one from: • whether they recovered; • their return to health; • their recovery from scurvy; • the effect after one week.	• A dependent variable is one which changes as a result of the changes made to the independent variables during the experimental procedure.	
(c)	1	Any one from: • there must be a different substance; • something in the fruits cures scurvy.	• A prediction is a statement that can be tested using an experiment. • The evidence in the question showed that it was not the acid which cured scurvy. It must have been something else in the fruit which cured this disease.	
(d)	1	Any one from: • effects due to diet may take more than a week to reveal themselves; • The body takes time to adjust to the diet; • time is needed for the results to reveal themselves; • the effects do not take place before the week; • the longer the time the more reliable the results.	• In order to make secure and valid conclusions it is important to be able to ensure that the changes in diet are actually those bringing about the observed or measured effects. • In this case you have to be sure which changes to diet are providing the cure for scurvy.	
Total	**5**			

Question 14

Part	Mark	Answer	Comments	What's this question looking for?
(a) (i)	1	water (H_2O)	• The two products of burning are water and carbon dioxide. • As these two gases pass through the U-tube made cold by the surrounding ice, the water condenses and becomes visible in the bottom of the tube.	*This question is testing your understanding of how elements combine through chemical reactions to form compounds and your ability to recognise that there are hazards in living things, materials and physical processes that have to be assessed and action taken to reduce them.*
(a) (ii)	1	carbon dioxide (CO_2)	• The two products of burning are water and carbon dioxide. • As the carbon dioxide passes though the limewater it reacts to produce an insoluble white solid which makes the liquid look cloudy.	
(b) (i)	1	Do not use antifreeze near a naked flame (it is flammable). Do not get antifreeze on your skin or in your mouth (it is poisonous).	• The two hazard warning symbols have specific meanings. Each picture should give you a good clue to the precautions you need to take. • Both correct answers are required for this mark.	See page 61 in Unit 3, Revision Session 6 of *Collins Revision Guide KS3 Science*
(b) (ii)	1 1	Any one from: • water froze; • the mixture froze; • the contents froze. **and** expanded.	• To get this mark you have to be specific that the contents of the wash-bottle froze; 'it froze' is not clear enough because this could refer to the wash-bottle itself. • Water is the only substance that expands when it freezes. The 10% solution is not strong enough to prevent the contents of the wash-bottle freezing at –14°C. On freezing it expands and bursts the bottle.	
Total	**5**			

Question 15

Part	Mark	Answer	Comments	What's this question looking for?
(a) (i)	1	The point at (60, 33) circled.	• The anomalous result is the one that does not appear to fit with the pattern in the data. • This point looks lower than it ought and does not fit with the gentle curve that could be drawn to join all of the points plotted on the graph.	*This question is testing your knowledge and understanding of some of the central aspects of Scientific Enquiry (Sc1); in particular the importance of considering and evaluating evidence especially when identifying and attempting to explain anomalies in observations and measurements.*
(a) (ii)	1	A smooth curve touching all points except the anomalous point at 60°C.	• The curve must be near or touch all points except the anomalous point. • To get the mark this must be a single line not a series of dot to dot lines and the line must not be so thick that the points are not visible.	

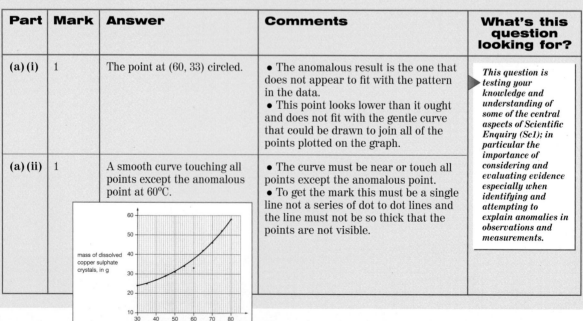

Part	Mark	Answer	Comments	What's this question looking for?
(a) (iii)	1	38	• Read the point where the line you have drawn on the graph crosses the vertical 60^{0}C line. • You will get the mark for any value of mass between 37 g and 39 g.	
(b)	1	Any one from: • They measured mass **or** temperature inaccurately; • They failed to make sure the solution was saturated; • The solution had cooled.	• To get this mark you must be specific and identify a mistake in the experimental procedure. • Stating that Sarah had not given enough time for the dissolving or did not stir the solution properly will also get the mark. • Answers referring to carelessness and writing things down inaccurately will not be specific enough to get the mark.	
Total	4			

Question 16

Part	Mark	Answer	Comments	What's this question looking for?
(a)	1	Any one from: • to prevent it collapsing; • to keep it open; • for support.	• The stiff cartilage in the wall of the trachea ensures that the opening into the lungs is kept open and that it is protected against collapse.	*This question is testing your knowledge of the role of the lung structure in gas exchange, including the effect of smoking and the ways in which some cells, including ciliated cells, are adapted to their functions.*
(b) (i)	1	gas A: oxygen (O_2) gas B: carbon dioxide (CO_2)	• Cells need oxygen for respiration. Oxygen enters the body through the alveolus into the blood and is then taken around the body. • Cells produce carbon dioxide during respiration. Carbon dioxide leaves the body from the blood through the alveolus. • Both correct answers are needed for the mark.	
(b) (ii)	1	Any one from: • it is thin; • it is one cell thick; • it is close to the blood supply.	• The alveolus is the site in the body for this exchange of gases to take place. It has a very thin wall close to the blood supply to allow the gases to pass from one side to the other.	
(c) (i)	1	Any one from: • it moves mucus; • it sweeps dust from the lungs; • it moves bacteria.	• These ciliated cells have small 'hairs' called cilia. These prevent mucus, dust and bacteria from sticking to the lining of the airway.	
(c) (ii)	1	Any one from: • it paralyses the cilia; • it stops the cilia working; • it clogs the cilia	• Cigarette smoke prevents the cilia from working properly and mucus, dust and bacteria will begin to accumulate in the airway.	
(c) (iii)	1	nicotine	• This is the name of the drug in cigarette smoke which causes addiction to smoking.	
Total	6			

Question 17

Part	Mark	Answer	Comments	What's this question looking for?
(a)	1	Any one from: • pieces are broken off; • the cliff is worn away; • it crumbles.	• Weathering is the general name given to the process that breaks rocks down into smaller pieces. • These are the visible signs of weathering taking place on a cliff.	*This question is testing your knowledge of the formation of rocks by processes that take place over different timescales and that the mode formation determines their texture and the minerals they contain.*
(b)(i)	1	Any one from: • remains or impressions of plants or animals which are very old; • remains or impressions of plants or animals in a rock; • remains or impressions of plants or animals or living things.	• Fossils are the outlines of previously living things which have been preserved in sedimentary rock as it has been formed. They are generally the hard parts of living things such as shells and bones.	See page 58 in Unit 3, Revision Session 5 of *Collins Revision Guide KS3 Science*
(b)(ii)	1	sedimentary	• Sandstone is one of those rocks which is formed by the deposition of rock fragments or organic material. This is the group of sedimentary rocks.	
(c)(i)	1	By the cooling of or crystallisation from magma or lava or molten rock.	• Igneous rocks are those that are formed from magma from within the Earth which reaches the surface through volcanoes and gaps in the Earth's crust and then solidifies.	
(c)(ii)	1	Any one from: • they are formed in conditions where plants or animals or living things could not exist; • magma is too hot for plants or animals to survive.	• The process of their formation means that igneous cannot contain fossils, as it is not possible for dead living things to be deposited in the rock and remain intact.	
(c)(iii)	1	Any one from: • larger in granite; • smallest in basalt.	• Crystals form in liquids as they freeze to become solids. • Rapid cooling results in the formation of small crystals and slow cooling results in larger crystals such as those of granite.	
Total	6			

Question 18

Part	Mark	Answer	Comments	What's this question looking for?
(a)	1	Chemical	• Energy is given out as the icing sugar burns. This is the energy stored in the chemical bonds within the substance.	*This question is testing your understanding of how the particle theory of matter can be used to explain the properties of solids, liquids and gases and how elements combine through chemical reactions to form compounds with a definite composition.*
	2	Any two from: • sound; • thermal (or heat); • kinetic (or movement); • light.	• The loud explosion produces thermal energy and light as well as being heard due to the sound produced. • Enough energy is transferred to the lid to cause it to move away rapidly from the tin.	

Part	Mark	Answer	Comments	What's this question looking for?
(b)	2	Any two from: • they gained energy; • they hit the lid with greater force; • they hit the lid more often.	• Energy gained from the explosion caused the gas molecules to move much faster and more of them hit the lid of the tin with more force.	See page 58 in Unit 3, Revision Session 5 of *Collins Revision Guide KS3 Science*
(c) (i)	1	Oxygen (O_2)	• When fuels burn in air they are oxidised using the oxygen present.	
(c) (ii)	1	Any one from: • carbon dioxide (CO_2); • water vapour (H_2O).	• When fuels burn, the carbon present is oxidised to carbon dioxide and the hydrogen present is oxidised to water.	
(d)	1	Any one from: • it was quieter; • the lid did not move as high; • less energy was released.	• From the table you can see that custard powder only produces 630 kJ per 100 g compared to icing sugar which produces 1680 kJ per 100 g. The result is a reaction which produces much less energy so less is available to be transferred into other energy forms such as sound and kinetic.	
Total	**8**			

THIS IS THE END OF THE TIER 3–6 PAPER

Question 19

Part	Mark	Answer	Comments	What's this question looking for?
(a)	2	Any two from: • bulbs are different; • different ages/resistances; • reading errors; • dirty contacts; • unreliable/inaccurate/faulty ammeter.	• Even though similar bulbs appear to be the same in all regards there are always minor differences between them, which means that readings may vary slightly.	*This question is testing your knowledge and understanding of some of the central aspects of Scientific Enquiry (Sc1); in particular the ways of considering different types of scientific evidence and how it is evaluated.*
(b)	1	0.75	• The current on A4 before the two extra bulbs were added was 0.45 A. With the addition of two bulbs, which each have 0.15 A passing through them, the total current passing is 0.45 A plus 0.30 A = 0.75 A.	
(c)			• The independent variable, time, is always plotted on the x-axis. The dependent variable, current in this case, is plotted on the y-axis. • Both axes must be labelled with the correct variable and unit to get the mark.	
	1	y-axis: current, in amps/A/mA x-axis: time, in hours		
	1	A line or curve from the top left to the bottom right.	• As the energy in the cell is used the current flowing in this circuit will reduce overnight.	
Total	**5**			

Question 20

Part	Mark	Answer	Comments	What's this question looking for?
(a)(i)	1	Only red light passes through the red filter.	• Coloured filters absorb all colours of white light except the colour of the filter, which can pass through.	*This question is testing your understanding of the effect of colour filters on white light and how coloured objects appear in white light and in other colours of light.*
	1	The red light is absorbed or stopped by the green filter.	• The red light is the only colour, which passes through the red filter, but the green filter absorbs it so no light reaches the screen.	
(a)(ii)	1	A circle of red light.	• Red light, which has passed through the hole in the green filter, forms a circle of red light on the screen.	*See page 100 in Unit 4, Revision Session 7 of Collins Revision Guide KS3 Science*
(b)(i)	1	red	• The red curtains appear this colour because they reflect any red light shone at them.	
(b)(ii)	1	The red light is reflected or scattered.	• The curtains appear red because they reflect red light. So all of the light from a red spotlight will be reflected or scattered from their surface.	
	1	The green light is absorbed by the curtains.	• Red objects absorb all other colours of light shone at them.	
Total	**6**			

Question 21

Part	Mark	Answer	Comments	What's this question looking for?
(a)	1	Any one from: • plants subjected to **or** not subjected to acid; • pH of the acid; • strength of solution; • volume of the acid.	• An independent variable is one which is changed during the experiment. • These are the factors which you can vary in your laboratory investigation.	*This question is testing your knowledge and understanding of some of the central aspects of Scientific Enquiry (Sc1); in particular the importance of ideas and evidence in science, the importance of planning in investigative work and how evidence is obtained and presented.*
(b)(i)	1	Any one from: • plants live **or** die; • plants healthy **or** not healthy; • plants **or** leaves change colour; • how many seeds grow.	• A dependent variable is one which changes as a result of the changes made to the independent variables during the experimental procedure. • Because you have to describe how you could measure this variable your answer to part (ii) must relate to the dependant variable which you write in this part.	
(b)(ii)	1	Any one from: • number of plants dying/ailing; • number of leaves falling/ailing; • mass of plant matter; • area of plant leaf growth; • height of plant.	• Your answer to parts (b)(i) and (b)(ii) must relate to the independent variable mentioned in part (a).	

Part	Mark	Answer	Comments	What's this question looking for?
(c)	1	Any one from: • soil nutrients; • temperature; • humidity; • light; • acidity of soil at the beginning.	• To make sure that what occurs is a direct result of changing the independent variables there are a range of factors which have to be controlled. • By doing this you can be sure that they are not causing the changes in the factors (dependant variables) which you are observing or measuring.	
Total	4			

Question 22

Part	Mark	Answer	Comments	What's this question looking for?
(a)(i)	2	Any two from: • light from the Sun; • reflected from the moon's surface; • travels from the moons to the eyes.	• The moons of Jupiter are visible because light from the Sun is reflected from their surfaces and that light reaches our eyes.	*This question is testing your knowledge of* • *the relative positions of the Earth, Sun and planets in the solar system;* • *the fact that the Sun and other stars are light sources;* • *the fact that planets and other bodies are seen by reflected light.* See page 70 in Unit 3, Revision Session 9 of *Collins Revision Guide KS3 Science*
(a)(ii)	1	Any two from: • they reflect different amounts of light; • they are not the same size; • they could be in the shadow of Jupiter or another moon.	• The brightness of the four moons can be quite different even though they are the same distance from the Earth. • The nature of each moon's surface could be quite different and this will affect how much light is reflected.	
(b)	1	0.68	• On the graph, from 3.6 (Earth days) on the y-axis read across to the line and then down to the distance from Jupiter (millions of km). • Take care with the scale on the x-axis – one small square is equal to 0.04 million km.	
(c)	1	the Sun the planets	• Galileo realised that the moons of Jupiter orbit that planet just like the planets of the solar system orbit the Sun. • Both answers are required to be awarded the one mark.	
Total	5			

Question 23

Part	Mark	Answer	Comments	What's this question looking for?
(a)(i)	1	magnesium zinc iron copper	• Magnesium reacts with the solutions of all three other metal salts. It must be the most reactive. • Copper does not react with any of the three other metal salts. It must be the least reactive. • Of the other two, zinc reacts with iron sulphate. Zinc is more reactive than iron.	*This question is testing your understanding of the displacement reactions that take place between metals and the solutions of salts of other metals and how the results of these reactions can be used to make predictions about other reactions.*
(a)(ii)	2		• Magnesium is more reactive than iron so there is no reaction between iron and magnesium sulphate. • Zinc is more reactive than copper so there will be a reaction between zinc and copper sulphate. • Magnesium is more reactive than zinc so there is no reaction between zinc and magnesium sulphate. • You will get one mark for each correct column in the table.	See page 97 in Unit 4, Revision Session 6 of *Collins Revision Guide KS3 Science*
(b)(i)	2	copper nitrate + silver	• Copper reacts with the silver nitrate solution and will displace the silver from the solution and combine with the nitrate to form copper nitrate. • The names of the products can be written in either order.	
(b)(ii)	1	copper silver platinum	• From part (i) you know that copper is more reactive than silver. • If platinum does not react with silver nitrate then silver is more reactive than platinum.	
(c)	1	Iron, because it is more reactive.	• Iron is more reactive than copper so any corrosion reaction will take place more quickly in those parts of the hot water system made from iron than in those parts made from copper. • Both the metal and the reason are required to be awarded the mark.	
Total	**7**			

Question 24

Part	Mark	Answer	Comments	What's this question looking for?
(a)	1	Any one from: • only a small sample; • insufficient evidence; • a bigger sample may have boys with green eyes; • they only tested boys in their class.	• If you look carefully at the table you will see that none of these boys had green eyes. • This conclusion is not justified because it is based only on the evidence from this group of ten pupils in this class.	*This question is testing your knowledge and understanding of some of the central aspects of Scientific Enquiry (Sc1); in particular the importance of planning in investigative work and considering whether the evidence is sufficient to support any conclusions and interpretations made.*
(b)	1	Any two from: • armspan; • handspan; • height; • mass.	• A discrete variable is a clearly defined difference in an observable characteristic. • Gender and eye colours are discrete variables. • A continuous variable is a difference which can be measured on a continuously changing scale. • Each of the variables in the table is measured on a continuous scale. • You must name two variables correctly to get the one mark.	
(c)	2	false true true cannot tell	• In graph C the shortest pupil is 144 cm in height but there are five pupils with hand spans smaller than or equal to the shortest pupil's hand span. • In graph B as hand span increases arm span increases. This strong correlation is demonstrated by all of the plotted points lying closest to a straight line. • If there is a high correlation between two variables they are likely to show a similar pattern of relationship with another variable. • You cannot tell if this is the case because gender is not plotted against height. Boys and girls are also not identified differently on any of the graphs which plot height against any other variable. • You will only get two marks if all four answers are correct. • You will get one mark if two or three answers are correct.	
Total	**4**			

THIS IS THE END OF THE TIER 5–7 PAPER

William Collins' dream of knowledge for all began with the publication of his first book in 1819. A self-educated mill worker, he not only enriched millions of lives, but also founded a flourishing publishing house. Today, staying true to this spirit, Collins books are packed with inspiration, innovation and practical expertise. They place you at the centre of a world of possibility and give you exactly what you need to explore it.

Collins. Do more.

Published by Collins
An imprint of HarperCollins*Publishers*
77–85 Fulham Palace Road
Hammersmith
London
W6 8JB

Browse the complete Collins catalogue at
www.collinseducation.com

© HarperCollins*Publishers* Ltd 2005

First published 2001
This new edition published 2006

10 9 8 7 6 5 4 3 2
ISBN-13 978 0 00 721543 0
ISBN-10 0 00 721543 6
Steven Goldsmith asserts the moral right to be identified as the author of this work.

British Library Cataloguing in Publication Data
A catalogue record for this book is available from the British Library

Edited by Jean Rustean
Production by Katie Butler
Design by Bob Vickers and Gecko Limited
Printed and bound by Printing Express, Hong Kong

Acknowledgements
The Author and Publishers are grateful to the following for permission to reproduce copyright material:
2000–2003 Key Stage 3 Science Test Questions, QCA

Illustrations
Qualifications and Curriculum Authority

Every effort has been made to contact the holders of copyright material, but if any have been inadvertently overlooked, the Publishers will be pleased to make the necessary arrangements at the first opportunity.

You might also like to visit:
www.harpercollins.co.uk
The book lover's website